Children, childhood and English society,
1880–1990

New Studies in Economic and Social History

Edited for the Economic History Society by
Michael Sanderson
University of East Anglia, Norwich

This series, specially commissioned by the Economic History Society, provides a guide to the current interpretations of the key themes of economic and social history in which advances have recently been made or in which there has been significant debate.

In recent times economic and social history has been one of the most flourishing areas of historical study. This has mirrored the increasing relevance of the economic and social sciences both in a student's choice of career and in forming a society at large more aware of the importance of these issues in their everyday lives. Moreover specialist interests in business, agricultural and welfare history, for example, have themselves burgeoned and there has been an increased interest in the economic development of the wider world. Stimulating as these scholarly developments have been for the specialist, the rapid advance of the subject and the quantity of new publications make it difficult for the reader to gain an overview of particular topics, let alone the whole field.

New Studies in Economic and Social History is intended for students and their teachers. It is designed to introduce them to fresh topics and to enable them to keep abreast of recent writing and debates. All the books in the series are written by a recognized authority in the subject, and the arguments and issues are set out in a critical but unpartisan fashion. The aim of the series is to survey the current state of scholarship, rather than to provide a set of pre-packaged conclusions.

The series has been edited since its inception in 1968 by Professors M. W. Flinn, T. C. Smout and L. A. Clarkson, and is currently edited by Dr Michael Sanderson. From 1968 it was published by Macmillan as Studies in Economic History, and after 1974 as Studies in Economic and Social History. From 1995 New Studies in Economic and Social History is being published on behalf of the Economic History Society by Cambridge University Press. This new series includes some of the titles previously published by Macmillan as well as new titles, and reflects the on-going development throughout the world of this rich seam of history.

For a full list of titles in print, please see the end of the book.

Children, childhood and English society, 1880–1990

Prepared for the Economic History Society by

Harry Hendrick

CAMBRIDGE
UNIVERSITY PRESS

PUBLISHED BY THE PRESS SYNDICATE OF THE UNIVERSITY OF CAMBRIDGE
The Pitt Building, Trumpington Street, Cambridge CB2 1RP, United Kingdom

CAMBRIDGE UNIVERSITY PRESS
The Edinburgh Building, Cambridge CB2 2RU, United Kingdom
40 West 20th Street, New York, NY 10011–4211, USA
10 Stamford Road, Oakleigh, Melbourne 3166, Australia

First published 1997

Printed in the United Kingdom at the University Press, Cambridge

Typeset in 10/12½ pt Monotype Plantin [SE]

A catalogue record for this book is available from the British Library

Library of Congress cataloguing in publication data

Hendrick, Harry.
    Children, childhood, and English society, 1880–1990 / prepared
for the Economic History Society by Harry Hendrick.
        p.   cm. – (New studies in economic and social history)
    Includes bibliographical references and index.
    ISBN 0 521 57253 3 (hb). – ISBN 0 521 57624 5 (pb)
    1. Children – England – History.   2. Children and adults – England
– History.   I. Economic History Society.   II. Title.   III. Series.
HQ767.87.H465   1997
305.23′0942–dc21   97-8907   CIP

ISBN 0 521 57253 3 hardback
ISBN 0 521 57624 5 paperback

Contents

Acknowledgements

I should like to thank Anne Digby and John Stewart for their advice and support. I am also indebted to the anonymous referee for perceptive and constructive criticisms. My main acknowledgement is to Michael Sanderson who, as editor, has been a model of assistance, courtesy and patience.

1
Introduction

Setting the scene

My intention in this book is to provide readers with a reliable guide to the growing literature on the history of children and childhood over the period from 1880 to 1990. By children, I mean the age range from babyhood up to thirteen/fourteen years; the survey has little to say about adolescents – fourteen to eighteen year olds – except in passing. Over the last twenty years or so historians have come to accept the legitimacy of young people's history. This is not to say that a large number of monographs are devoted *entirely* to children for, as a quick glance at the bibliography will make clear, there are relatively few such volumes. Rather it is that scholars have begun to pay attention to the historical presence of children as part of their wider concerns with, for example, the family, social policy, maternal welfare, women, demography and public health. However, as the subject area has yet to become a major focus of research, either in terms of prestige or of popularity, there is not that surfeit of historical controversy which surrounds so many other topics in this series. Consequently, although due attention is paid to scholarly dispute where it exists, the emphasis in what follows will be on describing and interpreting the results of recent research.

The theme under review here is amorphous, its discourse lacks theoretical rigour, and it has no well-established historiographical tradition which could be used to structure the survey. There is a risk that the information presented will be confusing and ungovernable. In order to avoid this situation, and by way of making each chapter more than a simple, self-contained entity, much of the material has been shaped into a form that can be described as 'age relations', meaning those sets of relationships existing between adults, in whatever capacity, and children. My hope is that this will provide a lens through which some of the most important changes, as well as continuities, in the relationships between 'children' and 'society' may be observed and understood.

Sources

There are no particularly distinctive sources to which scholars of the modern (post-1800) period in this subject area automatically gravitate, unlike, say, those available to economic, demographic or diplomatic historians. In general, researchers draw upon a body of materials that are widely used throughout the discipline of social history. Particular mention should be made of oral testimonies, which in recent years have become very popular in certain circles. The main division is between primary and secondary matter, with primary being subdivided into printed and manuscript items. The greater number of modern scholars have tended to use a vast array of printed primary sources, such as parliamentary papers, national and local government reports, contemporary books and pamphlets, the publications of professional associations and philanthropic societies, newspapers and specialist journals, and autobiographies. (The last can be especially important for the historian of childhood since many writers give full accounts 'recognizing this as a period when character and personality are formed' [1: *10–11*]). Turning to the principal manuscript sources, these include: government papers in the Public Record Office – those relating to education, juvenile delinquency, child protection, the School Medical Service and the wartime evacuation process; case and minute books of philanthropic bodies, such as the NSPCC; and local authority archival material on education, health and social welfare. Regardless of whether historians emphasize either printed or manuscript primary records, they always draw upon a range of secondary evidence taken from books, articles and biographies.

Almost all of these sources raise at least two difficulties for scholars. First, the majority were composed by the professional middle classes representing religious, philanthropic, medical, educational and governmental interests. This class bias is important since it is usually working-class children who have proved to be the most interesting subjects for research purposes, and yet few of the documents originate from within their social class. But this may not necessarily be much of an obstacle, for despite their outlook middle-class observers can make 'shrewd remarks' about social conditions and collect masses of factual material [2: *313*], which are open to interpretation by authors of opposing political persuasions. On the other hand, the fact that it is middle-class adults who make decisions concerning the contents of the collection does have to be borne in mind. Working-class children, were they to have the opportunity, might well make very different decisions.

Second, given that the sources have been written and compiled by *adults* – regardless of class – not only is the voice of the child more or less absent, but also there is always the related likelihood that the historian will be tempted to omit any representation of the child's viewpoint or, as frequently happens, even fail to recognize that such a perspective exists. Oral accounts are a partial exception to this exclusion in so far as something of the child's authentic voice may reach us via whispers and muted articulations, albeit that these are in the form of adult recollections.

Methodologies (concepts, techniques and 'forms of thought')

Since, as we have already noted, relatively few textbooks are devoted solely to the history of children, there has been almost no opportunity for scholars to develop specific methodological approaches and to debate associated issues. But why are children so neglected by historians? In order to answer this question it is worth remembering that in the past historians ignored the working class, women, black people, and lesbians and gay men. Since the 1960s, and much earlier in the case of the working class, each of these groups has begun to have a recorded history, largely as a result of their political struggles.

Children, however, lack a political significance: they do not have the vote nor do they have a political movement like feminism or socialism to represent their interests. Children are usually viewed from the perspective of *becoming* (growing to adult maturity), rather than *being* (children as their own persons). Similarly, 'childhood' as a stage in the life-cycle represents a wide range of physical and mental degrees of competence and knowledge: infancy, under five, primary school, secondary school, early adolescence. In this respect, 'childhood' is a fragmented experience. Moreover, individuals experience childhood for no more than a small part of their lives before growing out of it, unlike the members of other 'oppressed' classes. Thus only indirectly can it be said that there is a continuing children's constituency pressing for change. All this means that the political, social and legal status of children is very low on the agendas of political parties and in the academic writings of political and legal theorists. As children do not have overt political identities, historians tend not to be very interested in them as historical subjects, and certainly not as people in their own right.

For those of us who see ourselves as historians of childhood (and youth), one way forward is to draw two lessons (at least) from the methodologies and programmes of feminist historians [3–9]. First should be the giving to history of an 'age' dimension – as a 'fundamental category of analysis' – just as it now has a 'woman' and, in some areas, a 'gender' (meaning the binding together of men and women in the same historical story) dimension. This means putting 'children's history' into 'history'; the former cannot simply be 'added on' to the latter as if to fill in a gap. Moreover, since 'gender' brings together women and men, so 'age' must treat children in relation to adults, for conceptions of 'child' are never completely separate from those of 'adult'. Second, as women's history has been defined as 'critical history', so, too, should be that of children. The omission of children is ideological: it is a consequence of a set of attitudes and power structures. Writing the history of children, then, will involve confronting the politics of age relations.

Alternatively, numerous social scientific authors [10–20] have drawn upon the work of Michel Foucault, the French polymath, who in recent years has become very influential in a number of disciplines. The relevance of Foucault for our purposes is that whereas conventional liberal histories have tended to emphasize progress in the fields of child social and legal welfare and public health [2; 21–4], and other scholars have seen the whole process of 'reform' in social welfare, health and education in either Marxist and/or patriarchal terms [25–8], Foucauldian accounts examine what is called the 'regulatory impact' of these practices. This means that through welfare, health, education and legal provisions, children are 'monitored', 'surveyed' 'calculated' – nearly always in relation to their families – and that their health and welfare is fused with the broader political health of the nation.

Foucault rejects overarching structural theories of class and patriarchy to explain power and domination in favour of an approach that focuses on 'power' as 'knowledge', with the former being dispersed through, for example, science, law and education. He maintains that via the process of children being submitted to scrutiny, new forms of 'knowledge' are produced, primarily in the social sciences, which are then used to further regulate the children (and their families). This is accomplished via infant welfare schemes, school medical inspections, juvenile courts, child guidance clinics and social work with neglected and abused children. Thus regulation and control is imposed not by physical force but by the ability of those possessing 'knowledge' – doctors, teachers, lawyers, psychiatrists, probation officers, social workers – to determine what is acceptable, respectable and, above all, normal. By and large, those children who disobey, who are abnormal, are deemed to require 'treatment' (medical, psychological, social, educational) – sometimes together with their families – rather than punishment. Once successfully 'treated', they can be returned to the 'normality' of the normal family, so that they may have the opportunity of realizing their potential as future adults.

Of course, none of these methodologies – liberal, feminist, Marxist, Foucauldian – is mutually exclusive and, in practice, they often overlap with one another. Irrespective of which approach is drawn upon, however, we have surely reached the point where, with respect to children, the terms, standards and assumptions of what has passed for objective, neutral and universal history will have to be recast.

Aside from this issue, we need to be clear about the nature of the history of childhood which is advanced in subsequent chapters. Given that my brief is to come up to the 1980s, understandably much of what is said about the latter years cannot be based on 'historical research' because the written works have yet to appear and, therefore, this part of the review must be derived from other sources. To put it plainly, the period from 1880 to 1914 is fairly well covered in historical accounts, while the years between the First World War and 1945 have been much less discussed. None the less, there are a sufficient number of books and articles to warrant being included in this survey. When we come to the post-war era, however, with the exception of educational history, we are increasingly in the hands of social scientists, albeit that several have also written broad sweeping historical studies. This means that for the more recent times I have drawn upon methodologies and tractates culled from the work of child and social psychologists on patterns of childrearing [29–31]; social policy analysts on child care policy [16, 32–4]; health care specialists [11, 35, 36]; and anthropological and sociological theory and practice [37–41].

In the material presented here, which begins in 'the past' and ends in the 1980s, there is no clear division between 'history' and 'the present'. There are many historians who, quite properly, feel uneasy about this sort of thing, and they are especially uneasy about the forced coming together in such circumstances of historical data with those of social scientific research. Many historians are also often deeply suspicious of the language used by social scientists, which they see not as a specialist language, as in physics or chemistry, but as 'jargon'; so wherever sociological writings have been used in this book, I have translated many of the technical terms and phrases into my own words. For my part, however, provided the usual professional integrity with sources is maintained, I do not see a problem with the blurring of past and present in this context. This is not to say that I subscribe to a 'Whig' view of history, whereby the past is viewed through present-day categories. But it seems to me to be perfectly reasonable, after having made the usual caveats about the inadequacy of very contemporary sources, to present students with an essentially historical survey that concludes with references to our own time, so that they may see at a glance the broad pattern of change and continuity.

Notwithstanding the pros and cons of any particular methodology, in the following chapters, broadly speaking, five main 'languages' will be found, together with their associated forms of thought. First, the 'common-sense' view that by and large things have improved for children during the period. Secondly, an oral history perspective that is much more complex and very often acutely conscious of gender. Thirdly, a conventional social scientific viewpoint, dealing mainly with matters of child care policy. Fourthly, the Foucauldian method: critical and nuanced. And, finally, my own voice, which tries to look at things not from the viewpoint of class, gender or 'knowledge' but, informed by the different methodologies, from that of the children themselves or, as I like to put it, a voice that insists on the significance of 'age' in general and, in particular, on the lack of power that children experience in the age relationship.

The contents

Chapter 2 considers the new ideas concerning children and childhood in the late Victorian and Edwardian periods. The emphasis is on changes in the ways in which contemporaries were thinking about the nature of childhood, what it was, its significance, how it related to human evolution and, in a more directly political sense, how it should be defined in order to protect it for the benefit of the race. This was not the first time that ideas concerning children had been discussed but, given the new role of post-Darwinian science, the introduction of compulsory schooling and the pressing economic and political problems of these years, such ideas achieved a high profile and proved to have an enormous influence on successive generations of adults.

Chapter 3 looks at parent–child consanguinity. The first section examines four main issues around which an informed view of the topic has been produced for the decades between 1880 and 1920: family size and family economy, attitudes towards children's health and infant deaths, demands for obedience and methods of discipline and demonstrative affection coupled with parental interest in the child's world. The second section discusses relationships in a general manner, while focusing on child-rearing advice and social surveys of child-rearing practices. The reason for what might appear to be a somewhat arbitrary division lies in the previously mentioned relative neglect by historians of nearly all features of children's lives (especially their family lives) during the inter-war years and from 1945 onwards. In the absence of historical secondary sources, a range of social scientific matter has been employed.

Chapter 4 is a fairly substantial account of social policies involving children. There is a simple explanation for the length of the treatment given here: more has been written about this area of the history of children and childhood than any other. It is easy to see that, given the wide range of topics included in the term 'social policy', there is much to describe and discuss. Moreover, it is a particularly important subject for this book since it can be very revealing of the value placed upon children by 'society': parents, educationalists, health and welfare personnel, politicians, churchmen and assorted moralists. Reform programmes enacted in the name of children have rarely been as altruistic as the sponsors have claimed and yet, somewhat paradoxically, children have often been beneficiaries. The chapter begins by highlighting the work of several scholars as a way of introducing the most important overarching understandings of child welfare. It then moves on to illustrate these approaches through a chronological survey of legislation and developments.

In chapter 5 the connections between children, schooling and the classroom are discussed. There is a veritable mountain of literature on the history of education, the great majority of texts having little or nothing to do with children themselves. I have chosen to look at those areas that more directly involve children's experiences: the transition from wage earning and home-helping to school work in the late Victorian period, the early development of secondary education, mental testing and the 11+ examination, and classroom discipline. These subjects focus more overtly and less institutionally on the age relationship between children and society as mediated through schooling.

The subject matter of chapter 6 is children's leisure. This is a difficult subject to categorize. Although there are numerous studies of specific forms of recreation, the culture of children's leisure has barely begun to be examined. Consequently, this chapter simply surveys those activities provided by schools and by religious, voluntary and municipal organizations, as well as outdoor play, the cinema, literature, games, toys and television.

The conclusion, chapter 7, is a brief description of two issues currently the subject of much debate: 'disappearing' childhood and children's rights.

2
New ideas of childhood: the 1880s to the 1920s

There is a broad consensus among historians that during the late Victorian and Edwardian years new ideas or, in the language of social science, 'social constructions' of children and childhood gained currency and became widely acceptable social truths. The emphasis is on the word 'new', for this was not the first time that such ideas, perceptions, concepts – call them what you will – had undergone change. Classical scholars and medieval and early modern historians have also discussed the meanings and understandings of childhood for their respective periods [42–6]. And it is equally true that definitions of childhood, along with the relationships between children and society, changed repeatedly from the early 1700s through to the mid-nineteenth century under the following influences: the Enlightenment, the Rousseauian theory of Nature, the Industrial Revolution, the Romantics and the Evangelical revival [47, 48]. Consequently, the late nineteenth and early twentieth century developments were further stages in what was a continually shifting process.

But let us be clear as to the meaning of 'social construction'. This is an important term because much of what has been written about the history of children and childhood is the work of historians whose methodological framework, such as it is, has been influenced by social scientific writings, and of practising scholars in the social sciences. Put simply, the term refers to the way in which our lives and our institutions are *socially* produced, i.e. by ourselves, rather than naturally or divinely given. Childhood, then, 'as distinct from biological immaturity, is neither a natural nor universal feature of human groups but appears as a specific structural and cultural component of many societies'. In other words, though biological immaturity may be natural and universal, what particular societies make of such immaturity differs throughout time and between different cultures. So we say that it is socially constructed. Moreover, it 'is a variable of social analysis. It can never be entirely divorced from other variables such as class, gender, or ethnicity' [49: *8*]. This means that if we are to understand the nature of, and the relationships involving, childhood, we have to consider these other variables. None of this is to suggest that the condition of children is ever completely free of the biological dimension; nor is it to deny the effects of physical being, though the nature of the relationships that exist between the social, the psychological and the biological is extraordinarily problematic.

Whatever the difficulties, most scholars agree with Michael Anderson that 'ideas like parenthood and childhood are socially constructed and thus can be put together in [a] diverse set of ways' [50: *60*]. This is the view taken here. Acceptance of this premise means that the fresh concepts were the product of their particular historical situation. The purpose of this chapter is to provide a selective and mainly historiographical account of the emerging notions and, where possible, briefly indicate the reasons for, and the means by which, the 'diverse sets of ways' were 'put together'.

Viviana Zelizer, an American sociologist, has described what she calls the 'sacralization' (investing objects with sentimental or religious meaning) of American children between 1870 and 1930 [51]. During these years, the economic and sentimental value of children was transformed, and the emergence of this economically 'worthless' but emotionally 'priceless' child became what she calls the 'essential condition of contemporary childhood'. Her focus is on the way in which cultural factors have an independent effect on redefining the value of children. While not disputing that the 'expulsion of children from the "cash nexus"' was 'shaped by profound changes in the economic, occupational, and family structures', Zelizer claims that it was also part of 'a cultural process of "sacralization" of children's lives'. In the nineteenth century, the market value of children had been culturally acceptable (this refers to child labour); later, however, the new ideal of the child became that of an 'emotional and affective' asset which, regardless of social class, properly belonged in a world of cosy domesticity, school and play. Zelizer argues that where economic criteria had previously determined the 'value' of children, the twentieth-century child was priced 'exclusively by its sentimental worth' [51: *3, 11, 15*]. Here was a novel estimate of what childhood should be, and one that was by no means confined to the United States.

Another aspect of this tendency is evident in the work of John Sommerville, who portrays the dominant opinion of childhood in terms of standardization, by which he means the effects of education and social welfare, and demythology – the influence of Darwinian and post-Darwinian science in bringing about a new view of man and of the child [52]. Standardization involved providing 'a childhood for everyone, even if it meant squeezing some of them into the mould'. By the early 1900s this was being done institutionally through compulsory schools, youth groups, welfare provisions and the juvenile justice system [52: *189*]. In Sommerville's version, 'society' attempted to shape young people in accordance with its visionary model. Of course, 'society' does very little; it is usually social classes and groups within classes which establish such ideals. And there is little doubt that this ambitious plan originated in the middle-class attachment to certain notions of domesticity. It was essential to propose a proper childhood for every child, especially those of the poor, for this would help to prepare conditions for the spread of the nineteenth-century 'domestic ideal' – a concept which interpreted the 'domestic' in broad terms relating to political, economic, religious and cultural formations [53, 54].

The same insistence on the importance of historical specificity in identifying and explaining the creation of a more complex age relationship can also be found in the work of Hugh Cunningham who notes that 'childhood became inextricably implicated in the most critical public issues of the time'. A number of social surveys brought about the realization that children constituted a separate and significant section of the poor [55: *190–1*]; and 'child' study helped to categorize them [see below, p. 13]. But, 'underlying all these projects was a concern for the future of the nation and of the race, and children were seen as holding the key to both'. So it was that the public perception of them altered and, as they were moved centre stage, the movement to give all children a 'proper childhood' was well established [55: *191, 228–31*] by the end of the First World War.

The political and cultural struggle to extend the developing conception of childhood through all social classes, in effect to universalize it, has been stressed by other authors [48: *35*]. An essential factor in this process was the introduction of compulsory schooling in the 1870s and 1880s, which played a pivotal role in legitimizing the act of reconstruction [2; 48]. As Eric Hopkins has argued, the last quarter of the nineteenth century represents 'the classic period in which childhood was transformed', in that compulsory schooling replaced wage-earning as the accepted occupation for children aged five to around twelve or thirteen [2: *231*]. The significance of the classroom, and the entire ideological apparatus of education, lay partly in what was coming to be seen as the proper physical segregation of children from adults, and in its demand for 'a truly *national* childhood'. This in theory ignored all previous distinctions such as those arising out of divisions between the rural and urban worlds, the respectable and non-respectable working class, and the social classes themselves [48]. In addition, 'childhood' was not only to be national, but also natural – unpolluted by any form of precocity. This reflected an evolving attitude towards children, evident since the early 1800s, which held that they should all display innocence, vulnerability, ignorance and asexuality (as did those in the middle and upper classes – or so it was believed). The quality of 'naturalness' was essential to the making of what was consciously intended to be an all-embracing paradigm.

Equally decisive, however, was medical and psychomedical science, which provided the intellectual justification for the creation and identification of children's distinctive attributes, and for the concept of the natural. As several scholars have emphasized the role of science, it will be useful to elaborate on this in a little more detail [10; 26; 48; 47; 52; 56; 58–61]. In the eighteenth and nineteenth centuries young children had been objects of philosophical interest for experimenters who sought to reveal the presence or absence of 'innate ideas and qualities, or show the extent to which the attributes of humanity derived from sensations entering the sense organs'. However, in the period under consideration, science, though it played a crucial role in understanding children's minds and instincts, and the origins of juvenile delinquency, was perhaps more important for the role it bestowed upon the child in relation to human evolution, meaning that it looked to the study of children to reveal some of the processes by which the human race had matured. Nikolas Rose has described the scientific interest as follows: 'Observation of young children . . . might reveal the extent to which human emotions and expressions were inborn or learned. It might support the doctrines of recapitulation, for . . . the development of the child appeared to repeat the stages of the cultural evolution of humans from primitive to civilized. Time had become integral to the sciences of nature – why not to the sciences of man?' [15: *141–2*; 47: *169–70*; also 26: *43–59*]. By 1900 the doctrine of recapitulation was an unchallenged truth in child study circles [*57*] and, as such, it greatly contributed to the demythologizing trend. It was also an important influence on the ways in which the new ideas were being put together.

Similarly, David Armstrong, the medical sociologist, says that towards the end of the nineteenth century, the technology of social hygiene (that programme of social reform undertaken under the influence of medical and psychomedical science) invented the child as an object of medical interest. He draws attention to the *body* of the child, which became a focus of doctors' attention. This was partly through school medical inspection and, later on, also through the school clinic, and partly as a result of a general concern for the child's physical welfare as manifested by the selective school meals programme, which was administered by the LEAs from 1906 [10: *13*; also 12; 62; 63]. In this way, children entered what might be described as a kind of medical universe where they were given a specific status within the science, which served to 'invent' them as special beings who were significant figures in the larger national programme of social welfare. Moreover, this particular invention was itself part of a growing interest in their physical and mental features: in observing them, recording them, understanding them, and so on: 'Medical, scientific and political developments combined at the turn of the century to turn a floodlight of interest and anticipation on the small creatures hitherto left to tumble up together in their nurseries' [60: *98*].

One reason why political activists were inquiring into the nature of childhood is made clear by Carolyn Steedman who, in common with many other historians, sees children becoming the objects of legislative attention and forming 'the basis of various accounts of social development as they had not done before' [7: *62*; also 56; 62]. Steedman writes about childhood within the context of a biography of Margaret McMillan, the socialist propagandist and educationalist, who is seen as the 'translator of a wide range of physiological and psychological ideas into a coherent theory of childhood and socialism' in which children are used as 'symbols of social hope for a better future . . . as serious representatives of the human condition . . .'. [7: *4, 257–9*]. The outcome was a 're-making' of working-class childhood [58].

Steedman's account of the new idea of childhood is linked directly to the adult search (in this case a socialist search) for 'the path to a new world of social relations' [10: *4*]. She concludes: 'I recognise now how very little distinction we make . . . between real children and our fantasy children; that as we talk to, watch, teach and write about children, we want something from them, desire them: want the thing we can't have, which is our own past: our own lost childhood' [7: *257–9*]. We may query the accuracy of this provocative assertion, but it will be useful to keep in mind throughout this book that perceptions of children and childhood connect to adults as they search, in one way or another, for something – be it knowledge, happiness, power, security, wealth, innocence, comfort or peace.

This chapter has sought to identify and describe some of the major ideas relating to the meaning and nature of children and childhood during the period 1880–1914. There are two main reasons why we need to appreciate the significance of the roles played by social, political and economic forces in the process of transformation. First, the developments described in these pages were enormously influential in the making of a new relationship (perhaps we should say 'sets' of relationships) between adults and children, which has produced long-lasting and far-reaching consequences for all concerned. The second and more important reason is that in its entirety the transformation marked the conclusion to a complex pattern of evolution that had been emerging since the early eighteenth century and which, along the way, had yielded several overlapping, and often contradictory, interpretations of 'age' and its implications. The claim being made here is that the new ideas also heralded the beginnings of what can reasonably be termed 'modern childhood' in so far as between circa

1880 and 1914 childhood was in very large measure legally, legislatively, socially, medically, psychologically, educationally and politically institutionalized [48: *36*].

3

Parent–child relationships

Since the 1960s family history has become one of the most popular, productive and controversial areas in the development of social history. The debates and schools of thought were superbly summarized by Michael Anderson in an earlier survey in this series [50]. Unfortunately, his period extended only to 1914, which would seem to confirm that there is a paucity of studies covering the interwar and post-Second World War decades.

Anderson focused on three approaches: demography, sentiments and the household economy. Of these, the second is most relevant to this book since it specifically considers parenthood and childhood. Anderson claimed that the principal authors of this school were basically concerned with the emergence of 'modern' social relationships, a kind of present-minded history. Rather than examining change or stability in family structures, they were looking for changes in 'meanings'; in other words, they saw the family not as a reality but as an idea [50: 39].

We are not interested in the broader picture here, but Anderson does raise several points which are directly relevant to twentieth-century issues. First, in looking for trends in family relationships, we have to remember that 'in any group of the population more than one set of attitudes may be current at the same period', and that as attitudes do not change immediately, the 'old' and the 'new' may well exist together for a long time. Secondly, the sources used in trying to decipher the meanings behind attitudes are open to many different interpretations and have to be examined within a number of contexts: social, cultural, economic and political. Care also has to be taken in identifying a new attitude or behaviour pattern, for it could be that what is being observed is not new, but has only just begun to be noticed in the sources. Furthermore, certain sources give rise to problems of social class and professional bias, and this can be acute in looking at working-class child-rearing practices [50: 40–1]. Thirdly, and with specific reference to parent–child relations, 'given that behavioural changes occurred, how do we *interpret* them?' (my emphasis). Indeed, how can a behavioural pattern at any one time be interpreted? For instance, it has been famously claimed that in earlier centuries mothers were indifferent to the fate of their infants. Mothers who sent their babies out to nurse, 'did not *care*' [quoted in 50: 61]. This, says, Anderson, 'hints at a quite conscious set of mental processes'. Of course, as he shows, there are other possible explanations for the practice of out-nursing. One could be a belief that outnursing was safer than other alternatives to breast-feeding; another that outnursing was the product of family economic strategies that compelled mothers to be wage-earners in order to supplement the low wages of the male breadwinner. Fourthly, Anderson points to the issue of 'ideas' being the cause of social change. In opposition to those who believe that parental care is so curiously resistant to change [64: 271], Anderson accepts that significant reform has taken place in this and in other family relationships. However, the 'sentiments' historians see attitudinal and behavioural shifts as emanating from broader cultural trends, like market capitalism or changes in political, religious and philosophical thought. All this may sound plausible, says Anderson, but the 'actual impact' of these developments on family behaviour has never been satisfactorily demonstrated [50: 61–2].

In opposition to the 'sentiments' scholars, who are accused of overstressing cultural factors, and of ignoring changes in the political economy of the family, Anderson commends the household economic school for having highlighted the importance of economic factors in the changing emotional life of the family [50: 64–84]. This school is influenced by 'social-science-inspired theories about the patterning of social relationships and of change in relationships'. At the risk of oversimplifying what is a fairly complex approach, the emphasis is on the ways in which economic resources (including human resources) are generated and used, and on the power relationships to which these processes give rise. Familial behaviour is seen as a corollary of economic constraints, rather than as a simple matter of free choice.

1880s–1920s

Family size and economy

This is a vitally important area of discussion. It is what might be termed an overarching topic since the way in which it is resolved will affect the interpretation of the parent–child relationship. Let us begin with a reasonably neutral statement. There is little doubt that throughout our period there was an alteration and, almost certainly, an improvement in the different ways in which working-class and middle-class children were both regarded and treated by their parents. This was the product of two factors. First, allowing for social-class differentials, there was the decline in family size from an average of six children in the 1860s to three in the 1900s and two in the 1920s. While the 1870s are seen as something of a turning point, the reasons for the decline are complex and open to debate. Generally speaking, the explanation can be found in demographic, economic and sociological issues, such as the increasing cost of education, the decline in infant mortality, the emergence of basic state welfare provision for the elderly, the rising standard of living, and changes in attitudes and values like secularization and women's rights. There is no suggestion that the changing pattern of marital fertility was originally influenced by the desire to provide better treatment for children, except perhaps with respect to the social aspirations of middle-class parents for their sons [65: *chapter 5*; *66*; 67: *46*; 68: *11–32*]. The second factor was the rising standard of living, which resulted from regular and less physically debilitating jobs, increased wage rates, improved housing, garden space, domestic technology, varied leisure facilities and paid holidays [2: *chapter 9*; 1: *215–17*].

Paul Thompson, using evidence from a large-scale oral history project, suggests that there was a demographic background to the rise of 'progressive' child-rearing among sections of the middle class in the early 1900s, and that a parallel change occurred among the working class. Fewer children, he says, made the home less over-crowded and easier to keep clean; there was more time for individual affection and less pressure to impose strict discipline. What he calls the 'gentle, home-centred working-class family of two or three children', which would become increasingly common, could already be found in the early twentieth century [69: *289–90*; also 70: *60*]. That overcrowding and poverty encouraged rigid discipline, and that the most dramatic changes in styles of mothering occurred among the middle and upper classes, is also confirmed by other authors [71: *43, 50*], which suggests that child-rearing practices are conditioned not only by social class, but also by economic and demographic criteria.

John Burnett appears to contradict Thompson when he writes that autobiographical evidence does not support what he calls 'this class-selective view of child-rearing', at least in the nineteenth century. The happiest memories of child life seem to come from large working-class families which, by modern standards, had little in the way of either comfort or luxury. Burnett concedes that poverty and worries about feeding and clothing a large family no doubt blunted the emotions of parents to some degree, but he thinks it would be wrong to conclude that affection was necessarily less, or that there was less concern for children's health and welfare. Emotional investment in children, he says, should not be equated with economic investment [1: *16*; *56*]. However, he then goes on to say that 'the happiness and well-being of children was present to a varying extent in all classes *so far as economic resources permitted* [my emphasis], and that as family size began to decline . . . as few wives worked outside the home and few husbands drank excessively, gentler, more intimate and loving relationships were able to develop'. This seems to acknowledge that economic resources were an important influence on degrees of tenderness and affection. Furthermore, he implicitly brings social class into the picture when he describes the 'affectionate family' as being more likely to develop in a comfortable physical environment, where parents were intelligent and educated [1: *16*; *53–4*].

Another way of looking at the question of demographic and economic circumstances versus 'affection' is to consider the relationship in terms of instrumentality. Here the argument is that certainly during the late nineteenth and early twentieth centuries, the majority of working-class parents regarded their children in a manner largely conditioned by financial and labour considerations, without much of what nowadays would be regarded as expressions of feelings or sentiment. Even so, it must be stressed that there are differences of opinion among scholars as to whether such instrumentality can be taken to be exclusive of other more 'affectionate' attitudes and practices. Nevertheless, it is agreed that during this time the organization of the household was based on the notion of reciprocal rights and responsibilities: children could expect to be generally cared for in terms of food, clothing, shelter and education in return for which they were expected to contribute to the family economy through wage labour and help around the house as soon as they were old enough [1: 220]. In fundamental terms, the pattern was determined by parental knowledge of the economic importance of their children in both the short and the long term [6; 8; 63; 69; 70; 72; 73]. Working-class parents reared their children 'according to a set of psychological presuppositions' that greatly influenced the relationship between them. Consequently, love and discipline were given 'within the seldom articulated, generally unconscious framework of this generational economic calculus' [74: 158].

Ellen Ross also considers the economic functions inherent in the late Victorian and Edwardian parent–child relationship, albeit exclusively from the standpoint of the mother. Some mothers were caring, affectionate and playful, but these were 'only incidental qualities of good mothers'. A good mother 'was mainly a good worker' [72: 128; also 1: 229]. Ross agrees that working-class mothers, unlike those of the middle class, viewed their children from the perspective of the economic and human resources they either contributed or required. David Vincent is more blunt: 'children had to be both loved and economically exploited' [70: 60]. However, Ross reminds us that in non-urban cultures, children universally made a domestic and economic contribution to the family economy, and so it was for working-class children throughout Britain [72: 148–9; 1: 220]. Indeed, on the basis of this assertion it could be argued that the child's labour was directly related to it being 'loved': '"Working for" mother would earn her love and discharge the obligations incurred during the dependent years of babyhood' [72: 152–3]. The implication is that maternal affection was conditional upon children playing their expected roles in the economic calculus. This would appear to support the view that economic circumstances did influence both the level and the distribution of affection within families. But the last word should go to Vincent with his thoughtful conclusion: 'If we want to understand the process of change . . . we must discuss the problem as one of an evolving pattern of material and emotional considerations, neither ever dominant, the balance between them varying as between classes and over time' [70: *61*].

Attitudes towards children's health and infant deaths

Infant mortality rates (IMR) were highest in the densely populated areas of cities, which were also working-class ghettoes. In 1913, for example, the IMR for England and Wales was 108 under one year per 1,000 live births. Among the middle and upper classes the rate was 77, and for the infants of unskilled labourers it was 152. In general, the poorer the family the more likely were children of all ages to suffer from chronic bronchitis, pneumonia or pleurisy and to grow up to be less tall and sturdy than those from better-off families [74]. In such circumstances parents were familiar with sick, dying and dead children. As to their emotional responses, research findings are unclear. According to Elizabeth Roberts, 'Most women accepted the loss of their babies as a sad, but inevitable part of life . . . Equally, there were quite possibly a few women who welcomed the loss of a baby . . . "More so when you had more mouths to feed"' [8: *165*; also 70: *58*]. Ross, on the other hand, writes of 'heroic mothers . . . watching night after night over feverish children . . . battling against death itself' [72: *166*]. Whatever their feelings, these mothers said little in the way of regret at the moment of death; their expression was one of 'linguistic frugality' [72: *167*]. This raises the question of 'arguing from silence': if the subject does not speak of it, should we assume an absence of emotional pain?

In unravelling the complex attitudes of mothers towards the health and life-span of their infants it is important to appreciate that until well into this century 'newborns' (those in the first few weeks of life) were not usually viewed as persons and, therefore, were not always loved as 'children' [72: *184*]. It may well be that the death of 'newborns' was accepted with fatalism, but that the death of infants and other older children was experienced with pain and distress. Ross is aware of what anthropologists call 'selective neglect' whereby 'sickly children are selected at birth for neglectful mothering' [72: *179*, *185*]. This was apparently rare in Britain, though it could be the case that the practice was so deeply embedded in mothering that it was never formally named [72: *179*]. Moreover, 'attachment' studies indicate that sickly babies discourage maternal attachment and, therefore, mothers are perhaps distanced from them. Similarly, married women with several children were often reluctant to grow too attached to a new baby and would seek abortions in later pregnancies [72: *186*]. Using this and other anthropological research, Ross makes the important and provocative suggestion that 'material deprivation may structure mothering and calls into question notions of nurturance, attachment, and bonding as universal or biological' [72: *185*; cf. 64].

Obedience, discipline and punishment

One of the major themes in autobiographical writing is that of discipline: 'the code of behaviour which [children] were required to follow and the punishments imposed for transgressing it' [1: *47*]. The 'code of conduct' was usually set by the mother and enforced by both parents. As a generalization, it seems that the higher up the social scale the more parents controlled their children, in particular through defining what was forbidden, but that the lower the social class the greater the severity of physical punishment. The main areas of discipline involved 'keeping up appearances' and 'respectability', household duties, behaviour at mealtimes and control of play and of playmates [1: *48*].

There is no doubt about the extent of parental demands for obedience nor about the strictness of parental discipline, including corporal punishment [8; 69; 74; 75]. Within the family obedience meant respect and deference for parents, allowing them peace and quiet, the punctual performance of chores, and a sense of order [74]. For many parents among the unskilled classes, the home was the only place where they could act authoritatively; here at least the adult could be 'master'. But, as James Walvin has perceptively observed, there were political and religious dimensions to these parental demands since the inculcation of habits of obedience and deference to authority could help to cement social cohesion between the classes, just as it could maintain the virtues of domesticity [75: also 6; cf. next paragraph, references to 'conformist generation' and chapter 5 references to school discipline as a means of social class and age control]. Not that it was framed in a conspiratorial fashion; rather it was seen as something socially useful and God given: 'Children ought to be submissive to parental authority. To be submissive is to yield a willing and cheerful obedience. The child who disobeys his father and his mother is guilty of great sin' [quoted in 73: *102*]. Although this exhortation contained a large measure of cant, it more than approximated to social practice and, therefore, carried a powerful message.

In her study of working-class women growing up, Elizabeth Roberts observes that they 'did not spring into adult life ready-armed for the battle for survival'. Rather as children they were subjected to various socializing influences which fed into their role as adults. They had transmitted to them not only a class culture but also a body of rules to be learned about what was 'proper'. A cardinal rule was the habit of obedience, which they learned from an early age: 'Their own wills and desires had to be subordinated to those of their parents; they were expected to do as they were told, and the overwhelming evidence from both before and after the first world war is that they did exactly that.' Working-class children, it seems, accepted their parents' guidance in moral, social and ethical matters; just as they were brought up by a 'conforming and conformist generation', so they developed into one. Even babies and small children were expected to know the difference between right and wrong. Rarely would childish misdemeanours be dismissed with 'He was too young to understand'; 'She didn't know it was wrong', or 'You can't expect a baby to act differently'. Besides obedience, other rules to which children had to conform included no cheekiness or answering back, strict regulation of mealtime manners, returning home from play when expected, content of conversation, no swearing and no mention of sexual matters. The latter could often have devastating effects on girls who had started menstruating, as mothers passed on their own sexual prejudices to their daughters [8: *10–17*].

Discipline was usually enforced through either the threat or the practice of corporal punishment. But how widespread was it? Most scholars would agree that it 'featured large in the lives of most Victorian children' [75: *46*]. It is more than likely that violence towards children was particularly widespread among the poor where manners were firmly imposed [76]. Burnett's view that the severity of corporal punishment increased down the social scale is confirmed by Robert Roberts for Edwardian Salford. No one, he says, 'who spent his childhood in the slums . . . will easily forget the regular and often brutal assaults on some children perpetrated in the name of discipline' [76: *45*; also 1: *48*; 71: *43*]. Even Ellen Ross (who is most sympathetic to mothers) admits that London mothers 'were indeed tough on small children', though usually the most violent punishment was administered by fathers [72: *147 and 150*]. Other feminists seem to have little regard for the integrity of the child's body, writing of the same mothers' physical punishment of their children as 'hardly surprising under the circumstances' [77: *42*]. However, the child's point of view is not presented.

But it would be wrong to imagine that corporal punishment was confined to the poor. In the period 1890–1940, ordinary working-class parents in Lancashire slapped, caned and strapped their daughters (and no doubt their sons) with varying degrees of frequency [8: *12–13*], and this seems to have been the general practice, certainly up to 1914 [69: *41*] and perhaps well past this date. On the other hand, Paul Thompson claims that corporal punishment was less frequently used than is often supposed because parental authority was rarely openly challenged: 'He never hit us. Well, he'd no need to hit us with the telling off he gave us . . . He didn't tell us twice' [69: *66*; 8: *11*]. These oral testimonies also indicate that the extent of corporal punishment may have varied regionally, being less prevalent in rural areas than in the north and Midlands where 'there was . . . a more frequent use of slapping and also of severer forms of chastisement' [69: *66*; see also *68*].

Degrees of affection

Affection is one of those terms, like 'love', which is extraordinarily difficult to discuss in historical perspective. Interpretations are made difficult by the fact that parents may love, or care for, their children without showing them much affection; it may be present in a relationship but, for a number of reasons – anxiety, illness or lack of time – rarely be demonstrated. Onlookers, however, may judge the degree of affection entirely on the basis of visible demonstration, touching and verbal expression. Of course, many parents could well have felt 'responsible' for their children, out of a sense of duty or fatalism, without having the inclination to be affectionate towards them.

Although working-class parents were undoubtedly physically, and probably emotionally, closer to their children than were upper-class parents who attended to child care through nannies, nursemaids and public schools, there could still be 'distance' in the relationship, described by Robert Roberts, with particular reference to the lower working class, as a 'gulf', often manifesting itself through notions of respect. This division 'made a profound impression on the minds and social attitudes of millions of manual workers' and 'to ignore its influence is to distort any picture of working-class relationships in the first half of the twentieth century' [76: *50*]. (This can be seen as further evidence of the power of patterns of child-rearing to affect adult political and cultural values: 75: *101–2*; 8: *11*].)

If distance inhibited affection so did the emphasis on self-control, an attitude that was widespread among working-class families: 'None of us wears his heart on our sleeves. We was brought up to keep us moans and groans to ourselves'. Thompson feels that this attitude was commoner in the north where evangelical puritanism and the harshness of industrial conditions profoundly affected family life [69]. And yet, some contemporary observers spoke of the 'ferocious affection' of mothers for their sons [74: *160*]. Oral histories provide a variety of accounts, as do autobiographical studies [1: *53*]. One person remembers his mother as someone who 'when you came in from school she had her arms ready for you and she used to say, "Well, what have you done at school?".' Another recalled 'She . . . didn't like . . . what you'd call affection – we never used to kiss much.' Some respondents remembered the influence of time: 'I don't mean that we didn't get love. But there wasn't time for, you know, we were never fussed because nobody had the opportunity or the time' [74: *160*]. We are reminded of Ross's comment: 'A good mother was mainly a good worker' [72: *128*]. But some parents clearly made the necessary time: 'I'd always go to him with any troubles, and he used to listen . . . and when we sat on the couch like we did . . . he used to put his arm round my shoulders. We used to sit there sometimes of an evening, cuddled up to him' [69: *63*]. This should alert us to the risk that in seeking to explain the conduct of those parents, especially mothers, who, through force of circumstances, were irritable, indifferent and emotionally cold, we may either ignore or undervalue those who overcame the same circumstances to develop warm, affectionate and sensitive relationships with their children.

It is reasonable to say that up to the 1920s, affective individualism was most evident in the middle and artisan classes [1: *54*]. It may also be true as a generalization, to which there are numerous exceptions, that the larger the family, the lower the level of affection [1: *230*]. Furthermore, affection between fathers and their children seems to have been far more rare in comparison with that between mothers and children. Autobiographical evidence produces almost a stereotypical father-figure: frequently drunk, thoughtless, uncaring, bad-tempered and selfish 'but occasionally over-generous and sentimental', especially in poorer families. For many men, the brutality of the working environment served only to blunt their emotional attachment to their families [1: *233*; 69]. On the other hand, many autobiographers reported fathers who were attentive and playful and who devoted time to their children, especially – it seems – to their daughters. Among boys the relationship with their father might be based upon admiration for his strength, courage and knowledge. Often it was the mother who was portrayed as 'over-burdened with work, irritable, nagging and demanding' [1: *235*]. Thus children learned to censure themselves [8]. Elizabeth Roberts noted that very few of her Lancashire women respondents stressed or even mentioned physical affection and tenderness within the family, though all 'explicitly or implicitly' were conscious of a strong bond between themselves and their mothers [8: *25*]. Whether this bond was forged out of a sense of common destiny rather than any feelings of personal affection remains uncertain [78: *6*].

The most distant and formal parents were those in the upper classes, although they were more likely to reason with their children than to use corporal punishment. How true this was of the nannies is another matter. In these families the word most often used to describe the father was 'remoteness' [1: *233 and 236*]. One reason for the distance between parents and children was the presence of the nanny or nursemaid. The range of child care duties exercised by these professional carers varied, depending upon the size and status of the household. Usually the higher they were in social class the less time parents would spend with their children, being otherwise engaged in professional, philanthropic and social activities. The children would eat, sleep and play in their nurseries, being brought down to their parents at set times. In terms of emotional comfort, these children were as likely, if not more so, to find support and friendship in a servant as a parent [69: *62*; 1: *231–3*]. In such cases the mother often came to be idealized [79]. At the same time, an increasing number of middle-class mothers, especially those influenced by the child study movement, were spending more time in the nursery, watching over their children's physical and mental development, and allowing them to play throughout the house [8; 60; 67].

But what of Linda Pollock's scathing attack on those 'sentiments' historians who claimed that in earlier centuries parents were less loving and affectionate and more violent towards their children than in modern times? [64] With the help of sociobiological theory, the study of primates, and anthropology, Pollock believes in the benevolence of parents and asserts that 'Parents everywhere start off with infants whom they wish to raise to independent adulthood.' Other authors, however, have pointed to the controversial nature of sociobiology. How, they ask, can Pollock explain babies placed for adoption or the prevalence of infanticide [16: *16*]? Similarly, Pamela Horn dismisses her claim that 'Parents have always tried to do what is best for their children within the context of their culture' as 'a bland statement' which 'begs many questions'. As Horn says, 'To youngsters harshly disciplined . . . it was doubtless small consolation to know that this was taking place "within the context" of communal culture' [80: *46*; cf. 2: *2–3*]. Horn's sensitivity is rare among historians, many of whom are too quick to use both the 'cultural' and the 'particular historical context' arguments [6: *9*]) to underpin their sympathy for those parents and school teachers who 'exploited' and physically abused children in one way or another.

Perhaps the main weakness in Pollock's approach is that rather than open-mindedly *exploring* the pros and cons of what is an important and controversial argument, she trawls through diaries and autobiographies looking for confirmation of her view, without giving much interrogative attention either to the contents or to an analysis of cultural contexts (cf. [1; 8; 9; 70; 72]). Likewise, she tends to ignore the general feelings of children as well as their interpretation of parental attitudes and practices, as is evident from her conclusion: 'Our method of child care is by no means an easy system – one has only to witness the constant anxiety experienced by parents . . .' [64: *271*]. But 'child care' involves children, too, and what, one wonders, of *their* anxiety?

The 1920s onwards

What we think of as the traditional strict approach to child-rearing remained fairly widespread up to the 1940s, certainly among the working class. Even so, 'from the 1920s onwards a new, slightly more indulgent and intense, relationship with sons and daughters started to develop' [71: *49*]. This is not to say that there was a straightforward trend towards greater humanitarianism, if only because the period witnessed the rise of 'scientific' baby care, with its emphasis on rigid feeding, sleeping and toilet training routines. As usual, we should distinguish here between the practices of middle-class mothers and of those from the working class. The former began to spend more time with their children, partly as a result of the decline in the number of young women becoming nannies and nursemaids, together with the spread of domestic technology. Working-class mothers, on the other hand, at first no doubt largely unaware of the scientific trend in baby care, carried on much as their mothers had done, except for the important influences of improved housing and rising wage rates. In order for us to understand these and other inter-war patterns of mothering, we must look at theories of child care and at the emergence of what was soon to become a mass market in child care literature.

Beginning in the 1920s there developed two new approaches to child-rearing: one was relatively short lived; the other proved to be more persuasive over the long term (both had the presence of Freud in the background). The first was the 'scientific' method of baby care, 'mothercraft', which was associated with F. Truby King, a New Zealand doctor, who advocated breast feeding ('Breast-fed is best-fed'), toilet training and sleeping according to fixed timetables, and with John B. Watson, an American behavioural psychologist, who wanted mothers to rear superior children. In their pursuit of 'well-adjusted' babies, both men promoted practices that were disciplinarian and authoritarian, emphasizing 'habit training' (behaviourism); and furthermore, they demanded that mothers be intimately involved with the rearing of their babies, but with a minimum of tenderness [19; 60; 81–3]. Although few of these prescriptions were *entirely* new, it was now claimed that they had been scientifically validated [19: *179*].

The extent to which these programmes were adhered to by mothers is unknown, but it will be briefly considered below. For the moment, it is worth noting that the emphasis on breast feeding implied an important change from previous patterns of baby feeding, at least among the middle class. Traditionally working-class mothers had breast fed, but from the early 1900s they were increasingly making use of the more convenient tinned milk, particularly after the hot summer of 1911 encouraged the use of Glaxo's powdered product. Truby King warned of the alleged dangers in using what were often unhygienic bottles, which apparently contributed to the high infant mortality rates. Equally important, breast feeding would, he said, encourage a greater intimacy between mother and baby [19; 60; 83]. However, the overall objective of Truby King's method was not infant welfare as such, but the rearing of an efficient and emotionally well-balanced individual: 'lack of regularity in babyhood was held responsible, not only for hysteria, epilepsy and imbecility, but also other forms of degeneracy or conduct disorder in adults' [19: *178*; also 83].

The emphasis in Watson's behaviourist approach was on the psychology of habits: his methods aimed to produce children who never cried, who were well behaved and independent, and who ate and slept as directed [19; 60]. In fact, Watson wanted to create a model child suitable for the American way of life with its high regard for self-reliance and personal emotional adjustment [82: *146*]. This child also suited an age in which nannies were increasingly difficult to employ at a time when middle-class women were attempting to enter the labour market and, therefore, required obedient self-contained children amenable to routines. This child, remarks Christina Hardyment, 'would hardly notice if his parents were around or not' [60: *172*]. While both men stressed habit and regularity, Watson was far more emphatic about the 'dangers' of parental tenderness, which could lead to 'hypochondria, invalidism, the proliferation of nest habits and the "mother's boy" syndrome' [19: *180*].

Unsurprisingly, a similarity has been detected between the rigidity and coldness of 'scientific motherhood' and nineteenth-century evangelical exhortations against spoiling for fear of damnation [81]. The other influential and more long-term trend was associated with the 'new psychology', whose components included the nursery school movement (popular among the middle class because the schools were replacing nannies), educational psychology, psychoanalysis and child guidance, all of which combined to produce more liberal elements in the parent (usually middle class) – child relationship. The new psychology suggested that individual will, emotions, and passions 'were not simply fuel driving behaviour which was then to be controlled by conditioning'; they were part of a whole personality that could be in conflict with its environment. Where the behaviourists and the disciples of Truby King had resisted giving in to what babies 'wanted', as opposed to their 'needs', the nursery educationalists were far more sympathetic to infant pleasures. For example, Susan Isaacs, the influential psychologist, recommended giving thumb-sucking infants substitute pleasures, such as boiled sweets, rather than prohibiting or preventing them with mechanical restraints, as the behaviourists advocated. Moreover, the nursery movement emphasized the role of 'play' – messy and dirty – in child development, thereby allowing children more 'freedom'. And, in common with the child guidance clinics, Isaacs reinterpreted children's antisocial tendencies as 'emotional dilemmas' [14; 15; 19; 60; 81].

This particular inter-war tendency culminated in what has been called 'one of the landmarks in childcare literature', Anderson and Mary Aldrich's *Understand Your Baby* (1939), which opened up the way for the 'fun morality' of the post-war era: 'Parents were now required to adjust to the rhythm of the individual baby who was no longer to be allowed to lie awake in the small hours, screaming. Attitudes to toilet training, thumbsucking and sexual curiosity were more relaxed and the idea of a "natural timetable" introduced. As for cuddling, the *bête noire* of Watson, it became not only acceptable but essential' [19: *188*; also 60: *213*]. But the Aldrichs' book did not lead to a quick revision in child-rearing methods in Britain: 'in an atmosphere of regimentation and increasing state control of many aspects of life, mothers of all social classes began dutifully to follow the Truby King style baby-care methods of the clinics' [83: *55–6*].

Once the war was concluded, a new approach to child care was soon in evidence, marked by Benjamin Spock's *Common Sense Book of Baby and Child Care*, 1946 (sales of which were exceeded only by the bible), with its emphasis on reassurance of mothers who were to 'enjoy your baby', 'have fun' and respond to babies in an 'instinctive, "natural" way'. The old rigidity was about to be replaced by a friendly, relaxed tone which told mothers 'you know more than you think you do' [52; 71; 83]. Yet we have to be careful not to exaggerate the extent of the changes, for while it is generally true that the first half century witnessed the emergence of 'a new ideal of parenting and family life' [81], there were many exceptions of a regional and social class nature.

Child-rearing literature is always a significant indicator of certain societal attitudes towards children, irrespective of the degree to which parents follow the guidance. So if we are to understand the post-1945 changes it is necessary to be aware of the relationship between the advice on offer and political objectives. (This relationship has already been noted above with respect to Truby King and Watson in their attempts to produce 'mechanical babies' [82].) Other factors were also at work, but they took longer to manifest themselves. The influence of the 'new psychology' owed much to the First World War experiences that catalysed the beginnings of social and psychological movements which, in seeking to understand and explain human aggression, came to focus on 'children's emotions, motivation and resistances' [19: *184*]. At the risk of oversimplfying a complex group of developments, we can say that by the mid-1930s the growing antipathy towards behaviourism flowed in part from its failure to understand childhood aggression, unlike the new psychology and the nursery educationalists [15]. Aggression was once again of considerable political importance with the rise of Fascism and Nazism, coupled with the fear of Communism. In this atmosphere, 'habit' training and rigid timetables for children came to be associated with 'Prussianism' and totalitarianism [19: *190–1*].

Consequently, the impact of the Second World War was one of reaction against both Nazism and Stalinism as the new democratic emphasis guided social thinking on a variety of issues [60]. The reaction was particularly strong during the war in America where the influence of behaviourism (Watson) was undermined, and where numerous books espousing liberal child care methods were published [82]. The dominant theme in these works was reciprocity in the parent–child relationship, and the inculcation of child discipline through guidance and understanding. In Britain the likely effects of evacuation on children had been given medical and psychoanalytical consideration in 1939, and there developed from this an interest in mother–child separation, primarily through the writings of John Bowlby. In the post-war period Bowlby's work became extraordinarily influential, mainly because it could be used by the government in its pronatalist attempts to reconstruct family life [15; 26]. In the process, attention was no longer focused on understanding children's aggression, but on the necessity for continuous contact between mothers and their young children. 'Mothering' became 'a', if not 'the', central motif [19; 26; 60; 81; 82].

Although there have been a few historical accounts of post-war child-rearing practices [see 9; 71; 83], the most detailed investigation is the three-volume study by developmental psychologists John and Elizabeth Newson [29] (which can be supplemented with other psychosocial studies [30; 31; 82]). In examining the changes in child-rearing patterns, the Newsons suggest that there is greater certainty when discussing middle-class parents, since they are more likely to have read and to have been influenced by advice manuals [29: i, 236; also 9: 142]. So it follows that middle-class mothers interviewed in the 1960s and 1970s were 'more inclined than working-class ones to say they were using much the same methods as their own mothers' who had themselves been influenced during the 1930s and 1940s by progressive educationalists and psychoanalysts [29: i, 251–2].

In order to elicit an assessment of social change in child-rearing, the Newsons asked all their mothers 'Would you say you are bringing up your children the same way as you yourself were brought up, or differently?' While for some mothers 'the great and obvious change was in material standards of living', for others it was the tendency to move away from 'strict, even harsh discipline, and towards greater flexibility, which was the salient feature'. Equally important was the perceived greater freedom of speech in the relationship, occasionally deplored as 'cheekiness', but more often welcomed. Furthermore, many respondents emphasized that in addition to the relaxation of discipline, there was a new warmth and companionship in the present day relationships [early 1960s]. The Newsons, felt that this trend was the result of 'a more general change in the social background which makes it possible for families today to enjoy much more leisure time together'. This was helped by slum clearances and rehousing schemes, which gave families modern amenities. Regardless of whether or not the emphasis is put on economic and material factors, these mothers agreed that within the space of a single generation, important changes had come about in parent–child relationships [29: *i, 237–49*; also 9: *141–57*; 81; 30].

For instance, in the rearing of four year olds, most parents, including fathers who were becoming more active and intimate, expected to find 'fun' in parenthood, and they rejected extreme authoritarian methods in pursuit of their goal. Underlying much of the new morality was the parental desire to be friends with their children: 'Many parents remember with regret the psychological distance which separated them from their own more authoritarian parents, and hope to achieve a closer relationship with their own children' [29: *ii, 556–7*; also 83; 84].

Looking back a generation, to the children of the 1940s, it is possible through comments from these mothers to catch a glimpse of *their* childhood. A rather large number felt themselves to have been 'unloved in childhood' and, therefore, this became 'the focus of differences in upbringing'. Leaving aside the disposition of individual personality, the Newsons suggest, as have other authors for earlier periods, that there are social factors which perhaps prevent the free expression of affection. The mother who is 'anxiety ridden because of poverty becomes highly irritable, snaps at the child when she would prefer to caress him'. Similarly, the heavily overworked woman has to make a real effort simply 'to find time for the cuddling and comforting which a small child demands'. The old saying 'When poverty comes in at the door, love flies out of the window . . . may be true for the small child in the very practical terms of the attention and response he receives from his mother' [29: *i, 246–7*]. The implication here is that poverty *does* tend to adversely affect parental attitudes towards children [60: *226*].

After the Second World War there arose what Young and Willmott, sociological investigators, describe as 'a new kind of companionship between man and woman, reflecting a rise in the status of the young wife and children which is one of the great transformations of our time' [quoted in 9: *96*]. More precisely, parental attitudes seem to have mellowed towards older children as they came to be treated more as equals and companions [71]. Where younger children were concerned, there continued to be sharp class differences in the principles of child discipline with parents in the upper social groups 'more inclined *on principle* to use democratically based, highly verbal means of control', while those at the bottom end of the social scale were likely to use '*on principle* . . . a highly authoritarian, mainly non-verbal means of control, in which words are used more to threaten and bamboozle the child into obedience than to make him understand the rationale behind social behaviour' [29: *iii, 445*; also 84].

We should also note that parents (usually mothers) continue to make fairly extensive use of corporal punishment in the rearing of younger children. As late as 1989, in a random sample of 700 families, the Newsons found that 62 per cent of mothers admitted smacking their one-year-old babies and, when four year olds were considered, there was 'a massive majority of children who [got] a smack at least once a week, going up to six days a week' [85: *1, 4–5*]. The general picture has been confirmed by a recent study showing that about a third of four year olds and a quarter of seven year olds were hit more than once a week [86]. Such statistics cast doubt on the conclusion of Thompson [69] and Roberts [8] that corporal punishment was less frequently used (earlier in this century) than is often supposed. Alternatively, it may well be that these scholars are correct with reference to older children who had learned obedience through having been hit in one way or another when they were aged from one to seven years. The Newsons suggest that smacking decreases around the age of eleven.

Notwithstanding these statistics, and the class differentials noted by all commentators, it is broadly agreed that as this century has progressed, so more liberal or humane attitudes have prevailed. Among the reasons put forward to explain this change are improvements in all aspects of the standard of living, including the very important expansion of domestic living space, together with smaller families. There was also the 'new' psychology, the decline of those strict religious views that looked upon children as 'evil', coupled with the rise of educational theories that saw them as 'flowers' rather than as 'weeds' and an increasing, if grudging, respect for their rights and freedoms. Thus 'most children today have more friendly and intimate relationships with their parents' than would have been so early in the century [71: 59; also 1: 52; 9: 157; 235–6].

4

Children and social policies

Until recently historical studies of child health and welfare assumed a 'Whiggish' tone, that is, they usually saw legislative developments in terms of 'progress' – a continually improving position [23; 24]. (But not all scholars subscribed to this view [87] and, unsurprisingly, political histories of welfare offered more searching examinations [88].) Older histories, along with several current standard textbooks on social policy, tend to describe the gathering pace of the legislation in terms of what Jean Heywood calls 'the growth of state obligation towards the child' [24: 94; also 89–91]. Since the late 1970s, however, a new and more critical history has appeared, often influenced by Marxism, liberal radicalism, Foucauldian perspectives and, to a lesser extent, feminism [11; 14; 16–18; 26; 27; 32; 55; 92–7]. Most of these modern views, while not denying either a degree of legislative progress or the increasing role of the state, propose a more complex and varied set of causes and consequences, seeking as they do to be more precise and more analytical in their accounts.

Approaches

In order to illustrate the variety of 'overarching' understandings of child welfare, this section selects several approaches adopted by different scholars.

In pursuit of a broader conceptual framework, it has been tentatively suggested that the history of child welfare might be usefully examined through, on the one hand, two 'dualisms': bodies/minds and victims/threats and, on the other, through the notion of children as investments [59]. Taking its cue from Armstrong's claim that the body came to be the subject of 'various techniques of detail which analysed, monitored and fabricated it' [10: *3*] and from Bryan Turner's observation that 'the body is the location for the exercise of will over desire' [98: *180*], the argument is that much of the history of child welfare has been the imposition of adult will upon children's bodies through four primary forms: food and feeding (the School Meals Service); medical inspection and treatment (the School Medical Service, infant welfare clinics and the growth of paediatric medicine); the ordering of the body in movement and control of the tongue in speech (in Poor Law institutions, schools, orphanages, reformatories, child guidance clinics, hospitals, courts); and the punitive use of physical pain in welfare institutions such as schools and residential homes [*59*: *1–15*; for confirmation from a sociological/feminist perspective, see 99; 100].

The role of the body was of special importance during the period 1880 to 1918, partly through the work of the NSPCC [93; 101], but more significantly as the working-class child came to be 'known' through the observation, inspection and treatment of its body (medically and socially) by infant welfare personnel, and in the classroom after the introduction of compulsory education [16; 27; 62; 63; 96; 102]. For many scholars the child's body is an indispensable component of the Edwardian programme of national public health [10; 11; 14; 59; 63; 102]. And it has continued to be a central feature of numerous identities of childhood since that time – such as those arising from inter-war controversies around 'malnutrition' and the effects of unemployment on health and welfare [94; 103; 105] and from the emergence of paediatrics as a distinct branch of medicine, which accompanied the growing interest in children's diseases as peculiar to them alone rather than as adult diseases in children's bodies [10; 11; 106]. Furthermore, both 'the body' and images associated with it have also featured in debates since the 1960s on child poverty [107; 108], in the 'rediscovery' of child abuse beginning in the 1970s [97], and in the current anxiety about the health of poor children [35; 36; 99; 109].

Besides the emphasis on bodies, children were also being perceived through their minds/emotions. Roy Porter, the medical historian, has observed that the body in relation to mind 'differs notably according to century, class, circumstances and culture' [110: *218*]. We need to be sensitive to this warning as we trace the progress of the mind/emotion perception from the child study movement of the late nineteenth-century through to the child guidance clinics of the 1930s and beyond, as interests moved along a spectrum of psychosocial and psychoanalytical concerns, none of which were mutually exclusive. Among the interests and concerns were 'feeble-mindedness', causes of juvenile delinquency, developmental psychology, child-rearing advice, 'maladjustment', and post-1945 notions of maternal deprivation and 'bonding' within families. However, it should be stressed that it was not a question of two separate domains – body and mind – but rather that they came to be viewed together in order to constitute the child as a medico- and psychosocial being who inhabited a special position in the population [11; 14; 15; 19; 26; 57; 59; 99].

The second dualism, 'victims and threats', derives from sociolegal writings [111; 112], but is also influenced, if somewhat loosely, by sociological debates concerning the definition of social problems, in particular those associated with 'blaming the victim' and 'labelling theory' [111; 113]. The classic definition of the latter is that 'deviance is *not* a quality of the act a person commits but rather a consequence of the application by others of rules and sanctions to an "offender"' [114]. With reference to the history of child welfare, the argument is that children have traditionally been seen as 'threats', either because they were convicted delinquents, or because they were regarded as *potentially* threatening to society, usually as a result of some form of neglect – in effect when they were objectively 'victims' [59: *7–12*]. In practice it was not necessary to have committed a criminal offence, merely the possibility of doing so justified their being identified as a threat. In the words of an inter-war government report: 'there is little or no difference in character and needs between the neglected and the delinquent child . . . Neglect leads to delinquency and delinquency is often the direct outcome of neglect' [quoted in 111: *73*]. Further legislation and reports confirmed this view. Thus, as Eekelaar *et al.* have argued: 'the language of welfare rather than punishment is overtly being used to achieve the same ends as a penal regime: the protection of an existing order by the containment and, at least theoretically, reform of potentially disruptive citizens' [111: *73*; also 16].

Where children as investments are concerned, few historians would deny that this has been the dominant perception of them in the policy-making process, usually in relation to programmes of a racial, educational, familial, medical, social and political nature. It is well known that the period 1880–1914 witnessed a surge of interest in health and illness which expressed a political concern for the condition of the nation [11: 20]. As part of this concern, the rhetoric from the nineteenth-century child-saving movement, with its emphasis on a sentimental depiction of victims, was transformed into a 'medico-social discourse of children at risk that expanded the concepts of victimisation, exploitation and abuse' [115: 176–7; also 10; 12; 15]. As a consequence, children were moved towards the centre of the political agenda so that in 'saving the child', states had other motivations besides the child's welfare: 'concern about population levels; worry about the level of "civilization" of the masses; desire to breed a race capable of competing in the twentieth century' [47: 137; also 27; 59; 61; 96; 102]. Accordingly, Rose can claim with some certainty that the health, welfare and rearing of children have been linked to the destiny of the nation and the responsibilities of the state [15: 121].

Much less pronounced in the literature is an awareness of the importance of generation (or *age*) in the history of child welfare. While gender, social class and race are widely regarded as crucial to a proper analysis of social policy, *age* is almost entirely neglected [59: also 39]. Frost and Stein are among the few authors who recognize that within the context of 'the family as a power relationship' generation is a 'key dimension' and the child 'can have interests separate from the mother'. Consequently, their explanatory framework is broadly based on the theme of 'inequality as manifested in differences in social class, gender, ethnicity, (dis)ability and generation' [16: 7, 2].

Integral to this analysis is the view that children have become 'objects of welfare interventions', which can be explained by looking 'at the state–family relationship and how this has changed over time' [16: 9; also 11; 15; 39]. One example of this approach, provided by Jacques Donzelot, maintains that the relationship between families and the state has taken a particular gendered form primarily through an alliance between mothers and state agencies in pursuit of child health, education and development [18; for reference to a feminist critique, see 16: 8]. This means that through what is called the 'welfare apparatus', a 'supervisory' regime, staffed by welfare professionals, is created. Although ostensibly always 'caring', it has a coercive role that derives its authority from the law, and can, in extreme circumstances, impose its will upon both parents and children. Similarly, it has been argued that children are conventionally viewed through the concept of familialization, meaning 'the fusion of childhood into the family institution to such an extent that it becomes an inseparable unit, which obstructs the social visibility of its weaker parts as a separate entity'. Furthermore, in terms of welfare policies, the institution of the family is said to be subject to 'Covert control by the state' [39: 268; 279]. For these commentators, then, welfare cannot be explained simply as 'an expression of our collective goodwill' [16: 9].

For the final word on overarching approaches, we can turn to the analysis of Lorraine Fox Harding, a social policy theorist, who has examined historical and contemporary child care law and policy from four different 'value perspectives': *laissez-faire*; state paternalism; defence of the birth family; and children's rights [32]. The *laissez-faire* perspective is associated with patriarchy and advocates that the state intervene in family relationships only in extreme circumstances. It was common in the nineteenth century, and has enjoyed some revival in the late twentieth century. State paternalism refers to the growth of state intervention from the late nineteenth century onwards. In this perspective the intervention 'may be authoritarian and biological family bonds undervalued'. The defence of the birth family (and parents' rights) has become popular since the establishment of the welfare state in 1945, as the state has intervened in order to support the birth family which, in practice, has often meant assisting financially disadvantaged families. The children's rights perspective holds that the child should be treated as a subject, as an independent person with rights which 'in the extreme form of this position' are similar to adult rights. On occasions this perspective has been influential, but overall its effect on policy has been marginal.

Let us now seek to illustrate the 'approaches' through a chronological survey of the main legislative Acts, the determining trends and developments and, where appropriate, highlight scholarly differences of opinion.

1880–1918

All scholars agree that this was a critical period for child welfare programmes, and for the emergence of state social policies. How can so much legislative activity be explained? There is no easy answer to this question, and it would be a vulgar methodological procedure to look for a set of straightforward relationships. Instead, the heightened focus on children of all classes, especially those from the working class, has to be seen as part of a much larger interest in science and in social welfare, which was itself a response to that composition of economic, political, racial, imperial and social crises so well known to historians of the period [88–90; 116–21].

Recent work identifies a shift, beginning around the 1870s, from a simple concern with child reformation and rescue, usually by placing children in either philanthropic or Poor Law institutional care, to a far more complex notion and practice of welfare. The latter pursued the national interest in the broadest sense and, therefore, looked to children's physical and mental development, to their education, their protection from uncivilized and neglectful behaviour, and to their instruction in matters of hygiene, personal responsibility and 'citizenship'. In line with anxieties about poverty, the effects of slum life, foreign competition and 'national efficiency', these children were given a new social and political identity; they became, in the words of a contemporary reformer 'Children of the Nation' [59; also 16; 47].

Perhaps the first important locus of activity to emanate from the growing awareness of the social and scientific significance of children concerned infant welfare. The initial campaign focused on 'infant protection' from 'baby farmers' (women who took in infants to nurse or rear in exchange for payment). Broadly speaking, the reform movement concerned itself with the complex problem of 'infanticide', with community child care networks for working-class mothers, and with informal adoptions (there was no legal adoption until 1926). We have already noted Jean Heywood's view on the growth of protective legislation for children, in this instance a series of Acts (1872, 1897, 1908) to protect babies, often illegitimate, from being exploited 'as a means of private profit', although she does recognize that the root of much of the problem lay in the inadequate financial support given to single mothers [24: 94]. Other scholars link the problem to abortionist midwives and suggest that the practices of wet-nursing and baby-farming were closely related to infanticide [122; also 93]. Ellen Ross, however, who admits that London infants were 'being abandoned and killed at a slow but regular rate throughout the later nineteenth century' [72: *187*], stresses that murderous baby farmers, each of whom had a dozen or more babies, were a rarity and that the death rate of infants cared for by paid nurses was no higher than that of other groups of bottle-fed babies.

Even more worrying for contemporaries was the decline in the birth rate as it fell from 35.5 per 1,000 population in 1871–5 to 29.3 in 1896–1900; the largest fall in Europe (except for France). Imperialists in particular were anxious about the implications of the decline for the defence and administration of the Empire. But it was the rise in the infant mortality rate (IMR) from 146 per 1,000 live births in 1876 to 156 in 1897, alongside a decline in the general mortality rate, that raised the level of concern and anxiety among many political and medical groups [96]. Understanding the problem of infant mortality proved difficult. In general, politicians and medical personnel focused upon two issues: the feeding of infants and the promotion of mothering skills, known as 'mother-craft', which led to the opening of various kinds of infant welfare centres [27; 96]. The major development occurred in 1914 when the Local Government Board offered a grant in aid of local expenditure for maternity and child welfare. This made it possible for local authorities to take over voluntary centres, while the passing of the Maternity and Child Welfare Act in 1918 gave the local authorities powers to provide a range of services. The IMR had been falling since the early 1900s, and it fell sharply during the war (from 152: 1,000 in 1900 to 96: 1,000 in 1917). Accounting for the decline has proved controversial. The range of factors considered includes environmental and nutritional improvements (such as the rising standard of living, better housing and healthier dried milk powder), the promotion of breast feeding and the development of health visiting. As for the medical contribution to the decline, while some authors see improved medical attention for premature babies as playing a part, more recent research concludes that it was 'limited and late' [27: *107*; 123: *22–3*; also 72; *124–7*].

The issue of infant welfare has been of particular interest to feminist historians, who have written about the topic from the mothers' outlook [27; 72; 95; 124]. The emphasis on 'mothercraft' in the official programmes has particularly angered these scholars for two main reasons. First, it reinforced the view that the child was the mother's responsibility rather than a joint parental responsibility, while encouraging the view that the proper role of women was in the home looking after their babies. Second, it implied that mothers were ignorant, careless and often indifferent to the conditions of their infants. According to Jane Lewis, 'Attitudes and policies concerning poverty . . . ran counter to the demands of women's groups for direct economic assistance', as did their call for policies to deal with 'low levels of nutrition [and] the inability of women and children to afford medical treatment' [27: *17*]. Lewis argues strongly that given the government's promotion of the 'ideology of motherhood', neither 'changes in medical practice nor in social policy . . . can be assumed to have been benevolent' [27: *21*]. Deborah Dwork, on the other hand, claims that the feminists are too dependent upon the social control thesis. Regarding their analyses, she says, 'one begins to doubt the sincerity of official concern with the problem of infant mortality: everyone appears to have been more concerned with controlling women than saving babies' [96: *228*].

Although the pivotal role of the mother is acknowledged by certain sociomedical writers, they approach the issue through the Foucauldian notion of 'biopower', which means the power to control life 'in order to optimise the capacities of individuals and populations' [11; 13; 126]. This is achieved through submitting the body/ies to scrutiny, surveillance and numeration [11: *21*]. These scholars put the emphasis on seeing the infant welfare movement as a clear example of this process in action since infant care is said to be socially constructed as a 'medical problem' [12], instead of, say, as a problem of poverty. Moreover, as infant mortality was 'invented' – in the sense that infant deaths only appeared in the Census as 'infant mortality rate' in 1877 – it is argued that the appearance of this new statistic signified the emergence of the infant as an object of sociological and medical interest [128].

One revealing sidelight on the relationship between children and society, which also pointed to the developing state interest in all areas of child care, focused on the education of the 'handicapped' child. This matter came to public attention partly as a consequence of mass elementary education, and partly in response to the social and political issues arising from the 'condition of England' debate in the 1880s [62; 129; 130]. The Report of the Royal Commission on the Blind, the Deaf and the Dumb (1889) concluded that, if left uneducated, handicapped people, including 'the educable class of imbeciles', were likely to become a burden to the state by swelling 'the great torrent of pauperism'. Consequently, in 1893 the Elementary Education (Blind and Deaf Children) Act made it a duty for local education authorities (LEAs) to provide the children with an 'efficient and suitable' education. The situation for the otherwise physically handicapped, however, was much less enviable, with the main effort on their behalf being philanthropic until the 1918 Education Act compelled LEAs to provide for them.

Legislation for the mentally 'defective' child was politically controversial, for in an age of European imperial rivalries mental defectiveness was an important feature of the wide-ranging debates about racial deterioration, physical efficiency and eugenics (the science of proper breeding) [59: *90–3*]. The issue was first raised with reference to the condition of school pupils as revealed by compulsory attendance. However, a government committee on 'defective and epileptic' children (1896) had difficulty in defining the terms and the matter was left largely unresolved. None the less, in 1899 the Elementary Education (Defective and Epileptic Children) Act was passed, although the permissive nature of the Act meant that ten years later only 133 out of 228 LEAs were providing educational facilities for these pupils. In the eugenicist climate of the early 1900s there was an unsuccessful attempt to exclude 'mentally defective' children from the 1899 Act, since eugenicists saw normal education as pointless, preferring instead to provide vocational education in order to assist them to contribute towards their upkeep. It was 1914 before the 1899 Act was made obligatory on LEAs. While there has been some debate as to the extent to which Social Darwinism and the eugenics movement influenced policy for the mentally handicapped [14; 62; 130; 131], the important point is that more money was spent on reformatory and industrial schools than on schools for all the handicapped: 'The maintenance of law and order had financial priority over compassion for the physically and mentally disadvantaged' [130: *152*; also 62].

By the 1890s the government was turning its attention towards a much more complex issue: cruelty to children. In the closing decades of the century parental authority began to be reduced as it found itself in conflict with the state over such issues as infant life protection, compulsory schooling, and child rearing practices. Historians see the Prevention of Cruelty to Children Act, 1889, as representing a 'progressive' step forward in the humane treatment of children and in their protection by the state. They also agree that the work of the National Society for the Prevention of Cruelty to Children (NSPCC), incorporated in 1884, helped to establish in the public mind that children had 'rights' against their parents. All the same, the degree to which the NSPCC and the legislation was simultaneously concerned with attempting 'to patrol family life', and inculcating 'civilized' values, rather than simply to protect children, should not be underestimated [59; 93].

When, in 1881, Lord Shaftesbury, England's premier philanthopist, was first approached by a Liverpool clergyman for his support in promoting legislation to protect children against parental cruelty, he thought the matter 'of so private, internal and domestic a character as to be beyond the reach of legislation' [quoted in 91: 52]. But within three years he would help to start a London Society. This change of heart, and the interest of other leading reformers, can be explained with reference to the significance of the 1880s as a decade in which social distress, economic uncertainties, and political developments involving working-class consciousness were causing a shift in opinion among the philanthropic middle and upper classes. Many of them felt that the 'respectable' working class, and those who aspired to that status, were being undermined. It seemed that the ideal of the bourgeois family – self-contained, private, loving, religious, hierarchical and cultured – was at risk, especially from those families of Irish extraction who made up a large proportion of the urban poor. Child cruelty was one of the specific threats, exemplifying as it did irresponsibility, callousness and brutality [59: 51].

It was through the combined efforts of Thomas Agnew, a Liverpool merchant and banker, and Samuel Smith, the Liberal MP for the city, that the first Society was founded. On returning from a trip to New York in 1882, where he had come into contact with a Society for the Prevention of Cruelty to Children, Agnew approached Smith, who was active in the YMCA and in child emigration schemes, with the idea for such a Society in Liverpool. Soon afterwards Smith attended a meeting of the RSPCA where he converted a proposal for a dog's home into a call for the defence of children, and on 19 April, 1883, the Liverpool Society was established. By 1884 the Liverpool example had been followed in Bristol, Birmingham and London.

The credit for the passing of the 1889 Act is given to the London Society with its three-pronged campaign of 'legislative analysis, wrenching propaganda, and organised growth'. Their early experiences convinced members of the societies that child abuse included a range of offences, involving several different causes, few of which were adequately covered by the law. And they knew that a number of obstacles stood in the way of reform. Poor Law guardians were reluctant to punish parents for wilful neglect; women were unable to give evidence against their husbands; the father had an 'absolute right' to custody of his children; schoolteachers feared the abolition of their right to inflict corporal punishment upon pupils; the liquor trade objected to fines on the sale of alcohol to children; the Band of Hope temperance movement feared that clauses to restrict the employment of children would interfere with their use of juveniles in campaigns; and the Home Office was lukewarm, although it was interested in prosecuting neglectful parents and in curbing child street trading [93].

Several scholars tend to portray the NSPCC as unproblematically benevolent with references to the 'rousing of the public conscience', and to 'those whose life-work it was to protect those weaker than themselves' [22–4]. George Behlmer sees its roots as lying both in the 'slow spread of humane sentiment' and the creation of 'a new moral vision in which justice for the young took precedence over the claims of parenthood'. He also acknowledges that the architects of this vision succeeded 'by arguing that the security of the home demanded it. The Englishman's castle was to be breached for the good of the castle, and, ultimately, for the good of the Englishman as well. Thus, child savers laboured also to save parents' [93: *2–3, 16*]. Similarly, Harry Ferguson sees the Society and the protective legislation as being part of struggles which not only helped to create modern child protection practice, but also identified how neglectful and cruel parents should be 'judged, helped, punished, and treated' [132: *132*; also 101]. As he says, such parents began to feel 'the weight of new social practices and powers' which broke with 'traditional Victorian strategies of administering welfare, regulating households, and punishing deviations' [130: *126*]. It is, then, important to see the prevention of cruelty to children movement (including legal intervention in matters of juvenile sexuality through the raising of the age of consent to 16 (1885) and the punishment of incest (1908)) as part of a larger enterprise identified by Jose Harris, among others, as 'a major restructuring of the legal relations between husbands and wives, parents and children, the family and the state' [117: *75*].

The same sort of legal relations were also prominent in the *permissive* Acts allowing LEAs to feed necessitous school children (1906), and to provide for the medical inspection and treatment of all elementary pupils (1907). The first reform was extremely controversial because to many contemporaries it signified the ending of parental responsibility for the basic care of children. But it is not an issue that has aroused much disagreement among scholars, most of whom take the view that despite there having been various philanthropic schemes for feeding hungry children since at least the 1860s, and acknowledging the socialist campaigns for school meals at the end of the century [28; 133], the single most influential factor leading to legislation was the post-Boer war (1899–1902) 'national efficiency' movement. The 'efficiency group' (politicians, academics, journalists, professionals) were concerned about a wide range of issues relating to Britain's apparent declining status as a great military and economic power. However, central to their activities was the fear of racial deterioration, which gave the whole area of social reform the status of a respectable political question. With specific reference to young people, this transformation was greatly assisted by the Report of the Interdepartmental Committee on Physical Deterioration (1904), with its call for limited schemes of school feeding and school medical attention [88: *60*; also 96; 102; 118].

But not everyone is satisfied with this explanation. Roger Cooter refers approvingly to Dwork for locating a sense of unease about racial deterioration back in the mid-nineteenth century [61]. And, given that the child study movement developed out of a growing anxiety, from the 1860s onwards, about the health and efficiency of the population as a whole [57], it is clear that the effects of the Boer war need to be placed in perspective. This is especially so when the importance of the 'rediscovery of the condition of England question' in the 1880s is borne in mind, since it led to a number of investigations and soon became central to political debate [57; 62; 88]. The point being made by Cooter is that we need to pay much more attention to political and ideological goals in the history of child health and welfare. We should recognize that social policy initiatives were part of a wider socio-economic and cultural change [61: *4*] involving, for example, the ideology of the family, motherhood, an idealized 'childhood', and specific medical, political and economic interests. It was these concerns that legitimized the partial break with the *laissez-faire* approach to child-care policy, and which marked children out as 'England's most precious resource' [88; 32]). In this respect, state paternalism and child protection were joined together [32].

There is a certain amount of debate as to whether or not the establishment of the school medical service aroused much less controversy than did the school meals legislation. The old historical view, associated with Bentley Gilbert, that the service 'came peacefully because it came secretly' [88: *117*] has been rejected by younger scholars, who see the legislation as being fully discussed and understood by Parliament [102: *43–5*; 134; 135]. Likewise, his view that the growth of medical *treatment* was not fully appreciated by Parliament has also been contradicted [102: *61–4*; 136].

The origins of the service may be found in five areas: foreign examples; sanitation reform and public health concerns; the 'overpressure' controversy of the mid-1880s (the fear that children's health would be damaged by too much schoolwork); administrative and legislative developments in education since the 1890s; and fears of racial deterioration. While all these are relevant, it remains true that as with feeding hungry schoolchildren, 'the rather casual public interest in the health of schoolchildren suddenly became a widespread fear over the apparent physical deterioration of the British working class. A healthy working-class child was precious in a way he had not been before' [88: *120*; 14; 63; 96]. The development of inspection schemes was fairly rapid, but medical treatment in school clinics and hospitals had to overcome a considerable amount of institutional and medical hostility before the Education Act, 1918, imposed a 'duty' on LEAs to provide for the health and physical condition of all their children.

Another important feature of the changing relationship between the state and the family was developed in the Children Act, 1908. The creation of a separate juvenile justice system (the central feature of the Act), is said to have 'reflected a revolutionary change of attitude from the days when the young offender was regarded as a small adult, fully responsible for his crime'. The Act 'aimed at a more comprehensive and child-oriented legal system and at more generous and liberal provisions for children in all walks of life' [23: 492–4, 637; also 24; 32; 91]. Other scholars, though not denying its 'welfare' aspects, point more emphatically to different motivating sentiments behind the Act, the two most influential being the desire to better regulate families and children and the perception of children as a national asset in which investment was the prudent course [14; 16; 55]. Furthermore, sociolegal writers, who are concerned with the evolution of the 'welfare model' of juvenile justice, point out that as the juvenile court dealt with both the criminal child *and* the needy child and, therefore, fused the notions of depravation and deprivation, so the court itself 'became a *locus* for conflict and confusion' [16; 111; 137].

1918–1939

The undoubted rise in the standard of living between the wars has led several historians to write in terms of what Charles Webster has criticized as 'the "myth" of the Hungry Thirties' [141; 142]. Part of the difficulty in assessing children's health and welfare during the period is that different historians begin from different assumptions. It is true that all the relevant health statistics show a continuing 'improvement'. The infant mortality rate for England and Wales (IMR: usually seen as a significant indicator of general health) fell from 80:1,000 live births in 1920 to 53:1,000 in 1938. Similarly, among those under fifteen years of age, the death rate from scarlet fever, diphtheria, whooping cough and measles also declined dramatically. Equally significant was the increase in the height and weight of children, and the earlier onset of puberty. The reduction in ill-health and mortality was accredited by a contemporary survey to 'improvements in housing, sanitation, hygiene, and medical skill'. A better diet, brought about by rising real wages and cheaper food prices, was another crucial influence [138; 140; 141]. All the same, a number of scholars, in common with government critics during the 1930s, look behind the general statistical picture to cast doubt on both the efficacy and the comprehensive nature of inter-war welfare services [141; 142; 27; 94; 104; 144; also 102; 143].

Although the decline in the IMR seems to offer incontrovertible proof of an improvement in the standard of health, historians have debated the reliability and meaning of the statistics [127: *67–71*]. J. M. Winter tends to accept the official view that the economic depression had only a slight effect on the downward trend in infantile mortality. (However, he also points to the possibility of a higher IMR among children of mothers who were born during the worst years of the depression, thereby suggesting that the effects on health may have been delayed [125–6; 139–40].) Webster distrusts the official health figures and argues that the decline in the IMR during the 1930s was much less rapid than in previous decades and from 1940 onwards. Webster also claims that rather than use national statistics, a better guide to the effects of unemployment on infant mortality would be to take the rates for depressed areas. Such regions, he says, show a worsening IMR in the early 1930s [141–2].

One of the most controversial issues at the time concerned malnutrition and involved the extent to which school meals (both free and charged) – including milk – were provided [94: *102–3*]. No one denies that throughout the inter-war period there was a substantial increase in the number of children being fed, however the most rapid growth occurred in the provision of milk and nutritional supplements, such as cod liver oil [102: *121, 125*]. Government statistics claimed to show that whereas dietary deficiency had affected between 15 and 20 per cent of school children prior to 1914, by 1925 the figure had fallen to below 5 per cent, and during the period 1925–32 'malnutrition requiring treatment' fell to only 1 per cent of school pupils. Even within official circles these optimistic data were contested and remained so throughout the 1930s.

The three main criticisms of official statistics were, first, that different medical officers used different systems of classification; second, there was little connection between the nutritional classification and the identification process of malnourished children; and, third, the standards adopted by medical officers were subject to wide variation. There was also the problem of an incomplete knowledge of nutritional science. The government's response was to mount a huge propaganda campaign to convince the general public that there had been a decline in malnutrition and that there was no real connection between ill-health and unemployment [102: *130–6*; *103–4*; *139–42*].

In the mid-1980s, the weight of research seemed to tend towards the view that despite the undoubted improvements in conditions for the majority of working-class children, substantial numbers continued to experience severe and increasing deprivation through the effects of long-term unemployment [144: *119*; also 105]. This view has been qualified to a certain extent by the recent work of Bernard Harris who, using anthropometric data (heights and weights of individuals), has tried to measure child health in relation to unemployment and stature. He concludes that 'changes in the average rate of unemployment did have an effect on the average value of children's heights even though the strength of this relationship varied from area to area'. This, he says, identifies 'the importance of the local context within which unemployment occurred', since those with the highest levels of unemployment were also usually badly provided for in terms of social and health amenities [102: *140–2*].

With the controversy surrounding child health and welfare in mind, few scholars would disagree with Fox Harding when she declares that during the 1920s and 1930s, children were not a major focus of government policy [32]. None the less, government officials *were* enthusiastic about tackling juvenile delinquency. Indeed, it is a striking fact that the major piece of 'welfare' legislation for young people at this time was an Act based on the recommendations of a government committee whose main concern was with juvenile offenders [59; 145]. The Children and Young Persons Act, 1933, was a consolidating measure, the main provisions of which included the forging of a closer link between the care of delinquent and neglected children and LEAs; abolishing the distinction between reformatories and industrial schools as both were merged to become 'approved' schools; removing neglected children from the care of the Poor Law; amending the constitution and procedures of the juvenile court system; and broadening the definition of children being in need of care and protection. It has been claimed that the Act was concerned to make the welfare of the child a paramount concern [23: *495*], and that it set 'a standard of welfare and rehabilitation for the delinquent and the neglected children and those in need of care which had never previously been approached' [24: *130*]. In similar vein, Victor Bailey, an authority on the Act, rejects the view that the measures within it were 'designed as coercive instruments by the governing class' [145].

A very different view of the Act is proposed by Frost and Stein who see it as essentially 'a reactionary measure with no vision of prevention or indeed a return to a "rehabilitated" family' [16: *32*]. Humphries accepts that the authorities began to see the incarceration of erring children from respectable families as counter-productive, but this did not apply to those from families considered to be morally and physically degenerate [25: *213*]. Bailey, on the other hand, emphasizes the Act's recognition of the importance of the home environment which, in most cases, could be found in the *natural* home, under the supervision of a probation officer [145: *147*] (but he is probably excluding households which were viewed as being in need of rehabilitation). Rose agrees that domestic circumstances were seen as crucial, but says that was because they offered the best prospect for combating juvenile delinquency. Unlike Bailey, he emphasizes the disciplinary and control functions of the legislation [14: *171*]. Sociolegal writers, who focus on the nature of the legislation from the perspective of how it affected children, rather than parents, have argued that while the Act did offer greater care and protection to certain groups, it was at the expense of irredeemably intertwining them with other children who were regarded as 'virtually inseparable from delinquent children' [111: *75*]. Furthermore, it was the threat of delinquency that governed the legislation and which led in this Act, and in others, to the 'apparent disappearance of concern for child victims' [17: *223*].

When it comes to children's psychological well-being, there is little doubt that this was distinctly secondary [32]. All the same, the growing significance of psychosocial treatments, especially child guidance, needs to be considered [11; 14; 59; 145]. The movement got properly under way with the formation of the Child Guidance Council in 1927, though a few clinics had opened prior to this time; by the late 1930s progressive LEAs were funding their own clinics. The young clients were usually aged between eight and fourteen, and the commonest reason for referral was behaviour likely to bring them into conflict with authority, rather than proper delinquency. Children were rarely referred for emotional disturbances. However, when the children were diagnosed, the position was almost completely reversed. Diagnosis also revealed habit disorders such as speech defects, enuresis (bed wetting), and sleep and eating difficulties. The treatment was said to be of the order of 'commonsense conversation' rather than anything resembling psychoanalysis, which was viewed with some suspicion within the medical fraternity and by the general public [14; 59; 146].

The clinic was one of the most significant ways in which 'society' (in the form of psychiatrists, social workers, psychologists, educators, magistrates and penal administrators) came to 'know' children and to seek to 'adjust' them to what was regarded as normal behaviour. Here there developed what Rose calls 'a second institutional location [the juvenile court being the first] for this new way of thinking about and acting upon the child and the family'. The clinic would deal with a variety of disturbed children: 'backward children, nervous children, stammerers, liars, truants, the unmanageable, the neglected, and the delinquent. Within its precincts the troubles of childhood would be diagnosed, norms of adjustment and maladjustment would be produced and refined, and normalization would be undertaken.' And as such, it would become 'the centre of a web of preventive and therapeutic child welfare embracing the nursery, the home, the school, the playground, and the courts' [15: 154].

1939–1960s

The evacuation process, the first wave of which began in September 1989, saw 826,959 unaccompanied English and Welsh children, 523,670 mothers with pre-school children, and 7,000 handicapped children sent to reception areas in the South and South-West, the East and West Midlands, and North Wales. This mass movement of children gave rise to what Angus Calder has described as the English tendency to confuse manners with morals as children were accused of being infested, incontinent, bad mannered and ungrateful [147]. The memories of evacuees who were billeted with families are mixed, and though there is no doubt that many thousands of children suffered in such a way as to condition them adversely for the rest of their lives, many others recall kindness and affection and even love bestowed on them by their hosts [148–52].

In terms of health and welfare, evacuation revealed the wider influence of inter-war poverty in a way that the official statistical aggregates could no longer conceal. The Commission of the Churches reported: 'The country was undoubtedly electrified to discover the dirt, poverty and ignorance, particularly of home hygiene, that still exists in large towns' [quoted in 152: *140*]. The government at first simply reiterated the view that it had propounded throughout the 1930s, namely, that needy children were the responsibility of their parents. But this negative attitude changed under critical pressure and from late 1941 the number of children receiving school dinners increased dramatically [102: *156–60*]. Bob Holman has argued that the evacuation process aroused a new sense of compassion among the middle class, accompanied by a determination to take action to challenge poverty [152: *142*]. John Macnicol offers a different emphasis: 'Evacuation . . . marks the conceptual transition from the "social problem group" of the inter-war years to the "problem family" of the 1940s and 1950s . . . the latter [was] seen as amenable to character reform through intensive social work intervention' [151: *26*].

Whatever the motives behind them, welfare principles certainly came into prominence. In addition to specific influences, such as the development of child guidance services, the general significance of evacuation was threefold. First, it revealed the destitute circumstances of a substantial minority of children, as well as putting into context the extent to which inter-war housing schemes had failed to eradicate the slums with the attendant problems of overcrowding, verminous conditions, and lack of toilet and washing facilities. Second, it showed the variability of local authority provision in infant welfare clinics, nursery schools, health services, and educational opportunities. Third, it stimulated the expansion of statutory provision of a number of health and welfare services [102; 150; 152].

Perhaps the single most important consequence of evacuation was the centring of 'the family' in all future policies for children's welfare. Indeed, Heywood is not alone in claiming that after relative neglect during the inter-war years, it was the war itself which 'rediscovered for the nation the value of the family' [24: *133*], including the social significance of Macnicol's 'problem family'. In the inter-war period, deprived and delinquent children had often been cared for in institutions, which meant that 'the problem child and the problem parent had become separated, instead of connected entities' [24: *134*]. Now the war, in particular the lessons learned from the trauma of evacuees being separated from their families, provided the opportunity for a range of new social policies [15; 152].

In March 1945 the government appointed the Curtis Committee to be the first inquiry 'directed specifically to the care of children deprived of a normal home life'. The Report's findings led to the landmark Children Act, 1948, whose main principles were: the establishment of local authority Children's Departments (under the supervision of the Home Office); a new emphasis on boarding out in preference to residential homes; restoration of children in care to their natural parents; greater emphasis on adoption; and the partial responsibility of the Children's Departments for young offenders. The duty of local authority children's departments to restore the child to the natural parents as soon as possible emphasized the importance of family casework in the new service (this was a feature that expanded rapidly over the next twenty years). Ideally, and significantly, every child in care was to be treated as an individual, with access to the same facilities as any other child in the community, thereby removing the last shred of 'less eligibility' which had survived since the Poor Law Amendment Act of 1834. In broad terms, the Act initiated a child care service which tried to help those children 'whose homes had failed them; lessen or prevent the trauma of separation . . . or grossly inadequate parenting; provide substitute, family-type care whether in institutions or foster homes; forestall emotional stunting in institutions and give the children a better start in life than they would otherwise have had' [24; 34; 59; 152–3].

There is no doubt that the Act, although originally envisaged as not much more than 'a comparatively minor service for neglected and deprived children' [153: *vii*], turned out to be a significant piece of child welfare legislation, which has been unjustly neglected in standard histories of the welfare state [33]. If its meaning is to be fully appreciated, it has to be seen in relation to the series of post-war welfare statutes regarded as underpinning the Welfare State: the Family Allowances Act, 1945, the National Health Service Act (NHS), 1946, the National Insurance Act, 1946, and the National Assistance Act, 1948. With the passing of the NHS Act, the SMS, renamed the school health service, passed on many of its services to the NHS. As a consequence of these Acts, the deprived child and the failing parents were viewed as an interrelated whole, with the objective of the child care service being the restoration of the child to the family [23; 24; 34; 153].

Unsurprisingly, many commentators view the legislation as benign; it is regarded as part of a more comprehensive breaking down of class barriers and the transformation of political differences from those of ends to those of means. The 1948 Act is said to have strengthened and supported the family as never before albeit that the intention of the legislation of the 1940s was 'to impose middle-class values on the working class and thereby reinforce the tendency for class differences of family structure to diminish' [23: 651–3]. In Heywood's view the duty of a local authority to provide for the proper development of a child's character and abilities was 'perhaps unmatched for its humanity in all our legislation' [24; 158–9; see also 110: 185–6]. For Fox Harding, the Act 'reflected an entirely new ethos . . . [it] set new and higher standards of welfare for children in care' [54: 136–7].

Other scholars, however, tend to focus on the family within a broader political context. Four main reasons have been suggested to explain why the family was seen as crucial for effective child rearing. First there was growing concern about the reproductive rate of the population, described by a Mass Observation report as 'the coming problem for Western Civilisation', which produced a programme of pronatalism. Second, the Act's emphasis on the personal care of children reflected not simply the advice of the Curtis Report, but that of psychologists such as John Bowlby and Anna Freud who were concerned for children's healthy emotional development in post-war democracies. Bowlby's research pointed to the dangers of sudden and chaotic separation of small children from mother-figures and, therefore, emphasized emotional attachment, security and continuity. Third, the impact of child guidance contributed towards a view of the family, what Rose calls a 'therapeutic agent', as the perfect environment for future democratic citizens. Fourth, the experience of evacuation produced not greater bonding between the classes, but a more detailed understanding of the extent and consequences of physical and mental poverty, and the identification of 'problem' families [14–17; 26]. Of course, these interpretations do not deny the progressive features of the Act, but they place less emphasis on the humanitarian aspects, preferring instead to pay close attention to the interests and agendas of professional bodies, religious and moral pressure groups, industry and political parties, which are seen to have influenced the legislation and the subsequent development of local authority child care provision.

1960s–1980s

With the establishment of the child care service under the 1948 Act it soon became clear that child welfare could not be confined to those in care since the really difficult area involved *prevention*, that is, working with families in order to keep children from coming into care. Although preventive work was performed during the 1950s, it was not until the Children and Young Persons Act, 1963, that local authorities were given the duty to promote the welfare of children through such an approach. And even then, this was achieved by combining strategies for combating child neglect with those intended to counter juvenile delinquency [34].

The fear of juvenile delinquency had been the main concern of the Ingleby Report (1960), several of whose recommendations appeared in the 1963 Act. The report reflected professional interest in the *treatment* as opposed to the punishment model of juvenile justice as it dealt with deprivation and depravation [16]. Jacques Donzelot has argued that as 'welfare' permeated the judicial process with the social services collaborating with the courts, so the judicial influence was extended into the social life of children and their families [18: *105*]. (For a less critical view see [24; 33; 34].) Nevertheless, the Act confirmed that the focus of the 1948 Children Act, on meeting the needs of children in care, had shifted to providing support for families in order to avert the need for care and to prepare children for 'citizenship'. Thus the way was prepared for 'a family service' in which, under the Local Authority Social Services

Act, 1970, Children's Departments were merged into Social Services Departments.

The later Children and Young Persons Act, 1969, while retaining what Jean Packman calls 'a basic conservatism', drew heavily on the family-oriented approach with its emphasis on the 'treatment' of the delinquent through a 'more "welfare" oriented jurisdiction' [34; 154–5]. Wherever possible offending children were to be 'treated' in their own home, rather than prosecuted through the juvenile court. The intention was to reduce the number of offenders appearing in court by substituting 'care proceedings' for criminal prosecution – the court was to become a place of last resort. It is noticeable that once again there is a concentration on delinquency at the expense of cruelty and neglect. Indeed, child offenders were to be treated in almost exactly the same manner as those who were neglected in some way or another. In some respects this could be seen as a progressive and humanitarian attempt to understand the causes of delinquency. For John Pitts, however, the issues are those of class politics: 'The debate about justice versus welfare' was 'ultimately a debate about means rather than ends . . . Stripped of their philosophical and theoretical trappings the parliamentary politics of the 1960s concerned productivity and conformity' [155: *12*; also 111: *78*; 15: *175*].

By the end of the 1960s, a new problem had arrived: child abuse. At that time child physical abuse was regarded as being caused by individual pathology, i.e. the character or personality of the abusing parent. It was perceived as essentially a medical problem, with an emphasis on 'disease', 'treatment', 'identification' and 'prevention'. Matters began to change from the late 1970s, when theorists such as Nigel Parton began to open up a new understanding of the problem through a social structural analysis using contemporary conceptual perspectives drawn from the sociology of deviance. Parton, among others, claimed that debates about child abuse, though presented as being about technical and professional matters, were in fact political. Child abuse, he said, involved social inequality and poverty. Thus the medical model, in focusing on individual pathology, ignored the economic and social position of the family. Nor did it consider the wider institutional abuse of children through pollution, poor health services, and bad housing [97; also 16].

While Parton, and those who share his views, are explicitly sympathetic to children's separate interests from their parents, Fox Harding shrewdly observes that such defences of what is called the 'birth family' tend to 'de-emphasise the extent and seriousness of child abuse as an actual problem . . . The *actual* abuse of children and its effects are somewhat marginalised' [32: *124*]. In a later self-critical essay Parton acknowledged that one of the weaknesses of his earlier work was that it failed 'to recognize the child in child abuse' [156]. It has also been argued that social structural explanations of child abuse are incomplete because they fail to take account of 'ageism' and the generally low status of children throughout society, not least the widespread physical punishment to which they are habitually subjected. Furthermore, these explanations do not account for the relative absence of child abuse from the headlines between the early 1900s and its re-emergence in the 1960s [59].

The slowly developing interest in child abuse in the press and among professionals exploded with the report (1974) of an inquiry into the death of Maria Colwell – killed by her step-father – (the first of thirty-four into the deaths of children known to Social Services Departments between 1972 and 1987). It is universally held that this report established the issue as a major social problem and led to fundamental changes in policy and practice. The reactions to the case have been described as constituting a 'moral panic' – that is, child abuse was seen as 'a threat to societal values and interests' – which can be explained by contemporary debates about 'permissiveness' and the perceived fear of violence in society. The case was bound up with a multitude of concerns relating to the role of social workers, the nature of the welfare state, and the extent of liberalism and permissiveness throughout the social services in their dealings with the poor and the deviant. In effect, Maria Colwell was taken to be the innocent victim destroyed by alien forces that were threatening 'the British way of life': radical social workers, feminists, Marxists, divorcées, pro-abortionists, homosexuals, and all those in favour of anti-authoritarianism, pop culture, drugs, and sexual and social libertarianism. The panic, then, concerned far more than the risk of injury to children [97; also 16; 32; 101].

The Inquiry Report criticized the child care system for its failure to protect Maria Colwell, but it also implicitly criticized the policies, especially the emphasis given by child care workers to maintaining the 'natural' family through their adherence to the principle of the 'blood-tie'. Critics argued that in child care practice the focus on the child, which was prominent in 1948, had been blurred by the increasing attention paid to the maintenance of the 'natural' or 'birth' family. The killing of Maria in her 'natural' family more or less halted this policy. So it was that state paternalism was reintroduced in the later 1970s, with a greater emphasis on substitute care and on protecting children from their families. These sentiments, legislated in the Children Act, 1975, placed much more emphasis on the child's welfare, now to be given 'first consideration' [32–4].

The 1980s was a decade during which long-established tensions between public child care policy, parental responsibility and rights, and the jurisdiction of the state finally snapped. Fox Harding sees the decade as one 'in which both the paternalist and birth parent perspectives were in evidence, while *laissez-faire* and child liberation had a more minor influence' [32: 230]. With a somewhat different emphasis, Michael Freeman, a prominent family lawyer, sees the period as marked by a 'precipitate over-reliance on coercive measures' [157; 2]. The problem was generally perceived as one of a lack of proper balance between too much and too little intervention by social workers. Increasingly the call was made for a new *partnership* between parents and the state, especially after the Cleveland affair (1987), where a large number of children were compulsorily taken into care on the suspicion that they had been sexually abused by their parents (sexual abuse was *the* child protection issue from about 1984), and the subsequent report of the inquiry, published in 1988. English child care policy during these years has been described as an 'uneasy synthesis . . . a pragmatic response reflecting a number of different, often conflicting positions . . . laissez-faire, paternalism, the support of the family, and children's rights' [32: 224].

Where the Children Act, 1989, is concerned, Fox Harding claims that each of her four value perspectives can be found among its sections. She sees paternalism and defence of the birth family's rights as the most prominent, whereas for Freeman the 'non-interventionist strand in the Act' is seen as dominant. Notwithstanding this dispute, the Act is concerned with 'parental responsibility', 'support for children and families' and 'partnership' (between parents and the state), and it reiterates the Cleveland Inquiry's famous proclamation that 'the child is a person and not an object of concern'. The most fundamental of the new concepts introduced was the replacement of parental rights and duties by 'parental responsibility'. Besides a new emphasis on the family, the Act also introduced a number of new orders relating to family assistance, education supervision, emergency protection and child assessment. Children 'in need' were legislatively defined for the first time and they were recognized as legitimate participants in proceedings affecting their interests. The main provisions of the Act sought to bring together public and private law involving children in areas covering child care, child protection, wardship and divorce. Old concepts such as custody, care and control and access were abolished, as were 'voluntary care', custodianship or the assumption of parental rights, the 'place of safety' order and criminal care orders. In addition, the use of wardship by local authorities was restricted, while in divorce cases the court's ability to scrutinize arrangements for the care of children was reduced [32; 157; 159].

With respect to the broader area of the socio-economic welfare of children, there is widespread agreement among commentators and children's organizations that from the 1960s onwards a widening gulf has developed between the majority of children whose standard of living has risen and a substantial and growing minority who appear to be living in deepening poverty. Some of the causes of child poverty are the result of long-term economic trends, others relate more immediately to government policies throughout the 1980s. Moreover, 'Rising poverty, job insecurity, unequal shares in economic growth and changing family structures are affecting every child and every parent from all sections of society.' There has been a sixfold increase in divorce since the 1960s; an increase in the proportion of babies born out of wedlock since 1961 from 6 per cent to 32 per cent; 1 in 5 children live in single parent families now compared with 1 in 13 in the early 1970s; while the proportion of dependent children living in households with less than half the average net income rose from 1 in 10 to 1 in 3 between 1979 and 1992; and one million children are living in housing unfit for human habitation [160–11].

In the field of child health there had been a considerable improvement between 1945 and the mid 1970s; this was reflected in the decline of infant and child mortality, and in the improvement in children's heights and general condition. The main cause was obviously to be found in higher wage rates, full employment, state welfare services, the creation of the NHS and their development of new vaccines [102: *200–2*]. None the less, there were nagging doubts about Britain's falling position in the world infant mortality table, the mental condition of between 5 and 10 per cent of children, dental dilapidation, and domestic and road accidents. The Court Committee (1977), which enquired into child health services, felt that they had not responded sufficiently to the changing nature of health and disease. Moreover, the report expressed a 'profound anxiety about the state of child health in this country' [quoted in 109: *157*; 102: *202–3*]. Further studies, while agreeing that children were healthier in the 1970s than in the 1940s, pointed to serious social inequalities in all aspects of their fitness and argued that in explaining these a key concept was material deprivation. This was reiterated in the famous Black Report (1980) which, in the light of its depressing findings, argued (vainly) for 'the abolition of child poverty [to] be adopted as a national goal for the 1980s' [quoted in 59: *268*; also 35; 109]. Furthermore, a recent study (1991) has concluded that with reference to chronic illness and disability and handicap, which are regarded as crucial features of child health, 'The part played by medicine in the prevention and management of these conditions reveals mixed messages about how we value children'. Without for a moment disregarding the tremendous advances made in combating children's illnesses and in preventive medicine throughout the century, the consensus of opinion appears to be that in this field, as in so many other areas of social welfare, 'Children have not been a focus of policy' [35: *216, 210*; 162: *165*; also 39; 108–9].

5
Children, schooling and the classroom

Schooling has always involved much more than the accumulation of academic knowledge. It has been central to the processes by which childhood has been socially constructed and, therefore, its history has much to tell us about the nature of the relationship between children and society. The account given here will say something about 'how school must have seemed to the working-class boy or girl at the time' [2: 249]; but the main purpose of this chapter is to indicate a few of the ways in which society was attempting to affect children for any one of a number of reasons – disciplinary, political, professional, educational.

From wage to school labour

We have to remember that the majority of children were in receipt of a certain amount of schooling prior to the new legislation in the 1870s, but often for no more than a few years. After the 1870 Education Act, however, schooling gradually became an accepted stage in the whole process of growing up [2: 238]. During the period 1870–1914, the school leaving age was raised three times: to ten in 1870, to eleven in 1893, and to twelve in 1899 (in many rural areas the new minimum age was ignored). In 1900 local authorities were given powers to raise the age to fourteen, but they had little effect until after the passing of the 1918 Education Act. Enforcing this legislation among the poor, many of whose children were desperately needed as wage earners, was a major struggle for the authorities who sought to compel attendance by employing school attendance officers. The 'school board man' worked through a system of graded warnings, followed by court summonses. The outcome could result in the levying of fines on parents and, as a final resort for non-attenders, subjection to the brutal regimes of either residential truant or day industrial schools. The extent of opposition to compulsion can be gauged from statistics showing that in London alone, in the year ending March 1900, 28,836 summonses were issued before the number declined sharply thereafter [163: *49*].

It is worth noting that by compulsorily keeping children within the classroom, schooling lengthened the years of 'childhood', while simultaneously reinforcing notions of the characteristics that were said to constitute *proper* childhood, namely ignorance, innocence and dependence. In this way, the *concept* of childhood (especially for working-class children) was altered [59]. Indeed, there is plenty of truth in the claim made by David Wardle that the rise of formal schooling was 'accompanied by a change in attitude towards children so fundamental as to make it reasonable to say that childhood was invented in the eighteenth and nineteenth centuries' [164: *27*].

But, as Eric Hopkins and others have shown, what makes the late Victorian and Edwardian years such a classic period in the transformation of childhood is the substitution of 'schooling' for 'work' as the accepted occupation of boys and girls [2: *38, 231*]. We have to be careful how we understand this description of the transformation for, taken as it stands, it could be misleading. It is not the case that within the classroom labour ceased; rather it was that its nature changed from being essentially physical to being mainly mental. This can be seen happening if we consider the idea of 'social reproduction', which refers to the means whereby societies reproduce their social institutions and social structure. For instance, feminist sociology, in its analysis of family patriarchy, has portrayed children as being 'reproduced' in schools (and in homes) by adults. However, this is not something that simply happens *to* children, since for them to be school pupils, they must study a number of curriculum subjects, each of which demands mental and sometimes physical effort, and they must also subject themselves to a particular kind of disciplined regime. Consequently, children are not passive: they work at reproducing themselves through school labour [40: *160*; also 165].

Although the statistics showing the extent of child wage labour are very unreliable [55: *166*; also 2; 6; 63; 163], it looks as if by 1870 the percentage of children aged five to nine in England and Wales who were officially gainfully employed was less than 1 per cent of the age group. The percentage of occupied male children aged between ten and fourteen declined from 36.6 in 1851 to 18.3 in 1911, and from 19.9 to 10.4 for girls. Regardless of the numbers, there is no doubt that 'Children found the delay of their entry into the adult world of wage earners irksome, for until they achieved that status their opinion counted for little in many a working class home' [63: *211*]. Pamela Horn tells of William Edwards, a fen child in the 1870s who, after being ridiculed by field hands while on his way to school, '"used to get into the dykes and slink along out o' sight in case anybody should see me and laugh at me"' [166: *30*]. Similarly, Standish Meacham records how 'Family and friends expected them [children] to work as soon as the law allowed, and they themselves looked forward eagerly to doing so' [72: *175*; also 163]. Certainly, those children who worked for money were in the community, learning its customs, traditions, skills and rules. Schooling, however, tended to separate children from the community, changing their status from that of wage-earner to 'pupil' (more so for boys than for older girls who, although not 'wage-earners', were periodically 'needed at home' to assist with housework and child minding [6; 167]). In being excluded from paid labour – full-time, casual or seasonal – children, it has been claimed, were denied initiation into what R. L. Schnell perceptively calls 'socially significant activity', which has 'major human values' and is essential 'for the development of a sense of individual worth' [168: *10–11*; also 72: *158–60*].

The early development of working-class secondary education

Broadly speaking, the typical elementary school was an all-age school, providing basic instruction in reading, writing, arithmetic and religion, which kept pupils from the time they entered to when they left at age twelve, thirteen or fourteen, depending upon which standard they had reached. Elementary education in general was intended to serve what were deemed to be the limited needs of working-class children and was not seen as the first stage in a two-tier system with secondary education to follow. Secondary education, on the other hand, in the grammar schools, was designed for the needs of a fee-paying middle class. There was a small opportunity for working-class children to enter grammar schools through the scholarship system, although by 1900 there were only 5,500 such places available. By the late 1880s, however, many of the elementary schools had begun to develop 'higher grade' classes for clever working-class children whose progress had gone beyond the normal curriculum. In certain geographical areas the higher grades from a number of schools were collected together to form a separate 'higher grade school'. But such schools did not meet with universal approval. Aside from the fact that they were an illegal use of ratepayers' money, there was a growing fear among conservative and middle-class opinion that, with their ever broadening curriculum, they were both obscuring the sharp social class division between 'elementary' and 'secondary' education and coming to rival the grammar schools [28; 169; 170].

All this was to change with the 1902 Education Act. The convoluted events leading up to the Act are not our concern here. The essential point is that the thrust of the preceding debate and the subsequent legislation was, on the one hand, to prevent elementary schools from developing their curricula while, on the other, to create a distinctly separate system of grant-aided (from public funds) and fee-charging secondary education. This was to be primarily for middle- and lower middle-class children, many of whom were as young as seven or eight, but with procedures that would allow exceptionally clever working-class children to gain entrance through scholarships to the secondary (grammar) schools [28: *238, 241*; 171]. All the same, after 1902 a blurring of the division between elementary and secondary education remained in two forms. First, there were the central schools, so named in 1911, to be found mainly in London and offering a vocational and scientific curriculum, but one set below the secondary school standard; and, second, from 1913, junior technical schools, recruiting their pupils at thirteen or fourteen and offering a training in the skills required by local industries [169: *376*]. In addition, the Act abolished locally elected school boards, which had been responsible for administering elementary education, and transferred authority to county and county borough councils as local education authorities (LEAs) who were given powers to raise rate money to create new grammar schools.

The crucial figure in the establishment of the new system was Robert Morant, Permanent Secretary at the Board of Education, and an elitist representative of upper-class views who wished to propagate the public school ethos through provincial grammar schools [169: *370–2*; 170: *22–3*]. Scholars, while tending to agree that only the very talented working-class children ever reached these schools, offer differing emphases. Michael Sanderson portrays Morant as someone who wanted to turn the grammar schools into 'genuine ladders for working class children to reach the ancient universities', thereby creating 'possibilities of social mobility for the exceptionally able of the working classes' [170: *23*]. Eaglesham sees Morant as prescribing a training for 'followership' for the vast majority of children in elementary schools, with only 'exceptional' children being selected for the secondary schools [171: *51–4*; 172: *21–2*]. In Brian Simon's view, the purpose behind this new structure was simply to 'impose within the state supported system of English education an hierarchic structure of schooling corresponding to social class divisions' [28: *239*; also 169: *372*].

In 1907 a free place scheme was introduced whereby in order to qualify for a state grant, secondary schools had to take in, without charge, upwards of a quarter of their children from elementary schools. The children concerned had to pass an 'attainment test' (claimed not to be competitive) at age eleven. This marked a change in official thinking towards greater access for working-class children, but in practice by 1919–20 only 82,630 children had free places (not all of whom were working class) out of a total secondary school population of 282,005 [28: *270–1*]. Even so, Sanderson looks on the early 1900s as being 'of profound significance in the development of access to education' [170: *25*]. Gillian Sutherland is less enthusiastic, writing that the 'essentially horizontal stratification' of the old system had not been 'either seriously eroded or directly challenged by 1914' and that the small amount of mobility was used to reinforce the system with 'a new respectability' [62: *167*].

With only 9.5 per cent of children in state elementary schools going into secondary education, of whom only one-third were non-fee payers, the Hilton Young Report (1920) recommended (and achieved by 1927) that the proportion of free places should be raised to 40 per cent and, more radically, it suggested that virtually all children were capable of benefiting from some form of secondary schooling, after having passed a written and oral test. Moreover, by the 1920s, there was a growing demand from the Labour Party, which was becoming a serious political force, embodied in R. H. Tawney's *Secondary Education for All* (1922), and from the National Union of Teachers, for a more integrated system whereby elementary led on to secondary school, and for more access to grammar schools [169: 385–6; 170: 26; 62: *169*; *181–3*].

But it was the Hadow Report (1926) that really focused attention on the structure of the education system. The main features of the report were, first, that the term 'primary' should be substituted for 'elementary'; secondly, that primary education should end at about age eleven plus; thirdly, that a second stage should then begin, which would end at eighteen, sixteen plus or, for the majority, at fifteen plus; fourthly, that although all pupils would go on to the second stage, there would be different types of secondary education available; and fifthly, that all children would take the eleven plus (at the time only about 10 per cent of children did so) in order to ascertain the type of school most suitable to a child's abilities, and to determine who would be awarded a free place. With respect to the different types of secondary schools, Hadow proposed three main categories: the grammar school with its literary and scientific curriculum, the 'modern school' for 'practical' pupils, and 'senior classes' for those who remained within elementary schools. The majority of these proposals were gradually implemented during the 1930s [170: *27–8*; 62: *175–6*].

Mental testing and the eleven plus

Both the eleven plus and mental testing were part of the search for efficient methods of classifying, selecting and allocating children throughout the educational system [32; also 35]. This was not just a pedagogical exercise: it was steeped in political interests arising from the emergence of secondary education after the 1902 Education Act and the accompanying search for the realization of what would come to be known as the meritocratic ideal. This has proved to be controversial in the history of education.

During the 1930s the elementary school assumed a new role. From providing an 'elementary' education for the working-class child, the school came to be seen as 'the normal early stage of most children's education . . . it was now simply the primary step to a secondary level to follow' [170: *30*]. Consequently, the move from the elementary (renamed 'primary' after 1944) school to the 'post-primary' secondary school (or senior department in the elementary school) at the given age of eleven became crucially important for deciding the child's educational future. The minority of children, most of whom were middle class, would go on to the grammar school (those who failed the 'scholarship' – after 1944 the eleven plus – could go as fee payers), while the vast majority of working-class children, unable to afford fees and either having failed the test or not having been entered for it, would go on to other, less academic and less prestigious, forms of secondary education [62: *187*; also 170; 173]. The 1944 Education Act, which abolished fees for grammar schools, consolidated the importance of the eleven plus as the means of entry into the grammar school.

By 1914 'testing', known as 'educational psychometrics', was in place. At first it was mainly used to grade 'mentally defective' children, but by the 1920s intelligence testing became 'closely associated' with eleven plus testing and the selection of pupils for transfer from primary to grammar schools. Gillian Sutherland has shown that earlier histories exaggerated the extent of mental testing. While the eleven plus came to dominate the transition from primary to post-primary education, mental testing did not assume a dominant position within that process. Nevertheless, the fact that 'over half but under three-quarters of the LEAs' in 1919–39 did make use of mental testing [62: *189*] suggests the extent of this experience for the school child. Moreover, between 1944 and the advent of the comprehensive school [in the 1960s] they were 'inseparable' [170: *91*].

The importance of the tests lay in their power – through success or failure (and in the 1940s, 75 per cent of primary school leavers had failed) – to change children's lives. There are different views on the exact nature of this change. Sutherland expresses it cautiously when she writes that a strong performance in the eleven plus 'might alter, even determine the course of a child's life' [62: *187*]. Others are more condemnatory. Failure created boys who were 'sulky, vicious, less like boys than ruined men' and who 'hated school with a coarse, sullen hatred' [quoted in 170: *56*].

Contemporary opinion was under no illusion as to the importance of the eleven plus in segregating those who failed the examination, and of the inferiority of the secondary modern schools. Referring to pupils in these schools a correspondent to the *Times Educational Supplement* (23 March 1946) wrote that they 'are not to be trained for any of the significant activities of society. Thus a State system of education is seen as serving a threefold hierarchy [grammar, secondary and technical], the place of a child within which is to be decided at an age not later than 13' [quoted in 174: *46*].

The rhetoric of the 1944 Education Act was that each child would receive an education suitable to 'age, ability and aptitude'. By the late 1950s, criticism of the eleven plus was beginning to gather momentum: it was felt to be 'too uncertain and too final' [170: *61*; also 175], and a number of reports were particularly critical of intelligence tests. There was also criticism, though it was never unanimous, of the entire tripartite system of education, which many LEAs were beginning to heed. Besides unfair regional distribution of available places, it was increasingly felt that the home environment played an important role in determining the child's overall performance in the eleven plus, while the examination itself was unreliable in so far as the English part of the test gave an advantage to middle-class children from articulate and cultured backgrounds [176]. However, what really began to sway public (and political) opinion was the growing realization that to condemn 75 per cent of the population to failure at age eleven was not only unjust, but was also a catastrophic waste of the nation's potential talent at a time of intensifying foreign economic competition [175].

The most important concept underlying the whole debate was that of 'intelligence'. The concept was associated with Cyril Burt, an extremely influential psychologist in academic and governmental circles. In his words, 'intelligence' referred to 'innate, general, cognitive ability', which remained constant throughout the child's life, and which could be measured and was the product of hereditary factors. Moreover, the notion of intelligence supported another major hypothesis, namely the idea of a limited 'pool of ability': only a certain percentage of pupils were capable of benefiting from different levels of education, and these could be identified through mental testing [170: *90–6*; also 175].

Yet was the theory of 'intelligence' valid? As several scholars have observed, the belief in the hereditary nature of 'intelligence' was a very convenient justification for the existing social structure. It told middle-class parents that their children were likely to inherit their ability and that this would be developed through a grammar school education – which could be bought for them. Equally it explained why the lower classes were in less demanding jobs and why *their* children found it so hard to pass the examination for entry into the grammar school. Indeed, in the opinion of at least one researcher Burt's table of IQ according to occupations turned class into 'a biological phenomenon' [177; also 174]. Similarly, in Simon's view, 'Mass "intelligence" testing not only produced results justifying the existing system; it also underpinned a whole ideology inherited from the past, but one which would be projected into the future' [173: *248–9*].

Adrian Wooldridge, however, argues against condemning psychometrics as reactionary. Such an interpretation, he says, 'lacks both logical force and historical feeling . . . [it] . . . ignores intricacies of circumstances and context, sacrificing understanding for moral outrage, and mistaking consequences for intentions'. Those involved in testing were meritocrats 'rather than conservatives and reformers rather than reactionaries' (and he points out that the socialist tradition embraced the meritocratic ideal) [57: *164–5*]. Wooldridge obviously sees this ideal, which was encapsulated in the 1944 Act, as the victim of a concerted and largely successful (at least until the late 1970s) attack by Marxist and other radical sociologists from the mid-1950s onwards. Psychometry was denounced as 'an instrument of class oppression' and in its place came 'equality and community', or egalitarianism and environmentalism. The former became the objective of education and the latter was used to explain the relatively poor performance of working-class pupils.

The function of education has always been contested, governed as it is by political ideologies [170; 174]. Until the late nineteenth century the emphasis was on aristocratic dominance; by the end of the century it had shifted to the notion of a meritocracy, and this held sway in different forms and in varying degrees until the 1960s when egalitarianism gained the ascendancy [164]. But the labour demands of a changing economy, as the Crowther Report (1959) made clear, should not be overlooked here. So it was that the movement for comprehensive schools began to find favour with politicians and the general public, though staunch critics remained. Unfortunately, the new comprehensives were built in areas of working-class population (post-war housing estates), while grammar schools were strong in middle-class areas [174]. In theory Britain had a developing system of comprehensive education, but in practice the grammar schools remained and their coexistence posed problems throughout the period, especially in so far as they were able to cream off the most academically able pupils in their areas. Moreover, comprehensive education got under way as relations between all those involved – government, parents, teachers, LEAs and children – became subject throughout the 1970s and 1980s to intense power struggles over objectives and practices [57].

But the fundamental problem facing those who sought to promote egalitarianism through education was to be found in what Sanderson describes as 'those characteristics of disadvantage in society at large which affected children's response to education' [170: *64*]. Investigations in the 1960s found little evidence that comprehensive education would modify the connection between social class and educational achievement [170: *64*; also 174: *202*; 57: *359*]. At that time, however, in a period of some optimism, this was an unpalatable conclusion and, therefore, it was largely ignored.

For Sanderson and Wooldridge, though, the real issue is Britain's economic competitiveness [176: *390*]. Wooldridge concludes with a call to bear in mind that 'Shortages of brain power prevent growth, supplies of brain power fuel it. More than ever policy makers need to know about the natural talents of the population . . . We must take talents seriously, not ignore them; encourage individual differences, not suppress them . . .' [57: *407, 420*]. This is countered by Simon (a Marxist historian), who sees selection in terms of social engineering. The reason for the reintroduction of testing in the 1980s, in his view, was to cope with overeducation in a shrinking job market. He quotes a senior DES official: 'There has to be selection because we are beginning to create aspirations which society cannot match . . . People must be educated once more to know their place' [quoted in 178: *504*]. Whichever view we take, it is important to understand that in the relationship between children and society, schooling is about far more than individual fulfilment.

Classroom discipline

Schools have always been socializing institutions, concerning themselves with the manners and morals of their pupils (and, by implication, of their parents) in the widest sense. In 1885, the regulations of an Oxford school warned: 'All children must come clean, and with their hair combed, and must bring pocket handkerchiefs' [179: *20*]. It is no exaggeration to say that schools were regarded by the ruling class as 'beacons of civilization'. Discipline and order in school, as Anna Davin shows, 'were about discipline and order in society. They were about class' [6: *131, 133*]. It could be said they were also about imposing on children their subservient role in the age relationship. Some authors seem to be overawed with admiration for what was apparently achieved. David Wardle finds remarkable the schools' success in civilizing children and he quotes William Ashworth, the economic historian, who eulogizes that as a result of schooling 'very few children grew up in a state of complete savagery, and that almost all of them were introduced to habits of discipline and order . . . they were at least taught to sit still, a lesson not without benefit to industry and to society' [164: *97*].

Such uncritical admiration for social class and age discipline is not universal among scholars. Lionel Rose is one of several historians who have noted an emphasis on the coercive aspect of education, pointing out that through regimentation, drill and corporal punishment, 'children were taught not only their place as children, but were also taught their future proper place as future adults'. The children were intended to be clerks, factory workers, labourers and domestic servants. In rural schools, the hierarchical tradition was even more firmly implanted, often through the cane [92: *134*; also 1; 6; 75]. Within the classroom children experienced a conscious policy of 'punctuality, cleanliness, obedience and silence, all sanctioned by sharp and painful punishments' [92: *185*; also 1; 6; 25].

In teachers' training colleges some attention was paid to teaching lesson preparation and presentation and to the manner of the teacher towards the children [63]. But the reality of everyday life in the classroom is said to have militated against the practice of well-intentioned principles [180]. On the other hand, perhaps the spread of humanitarian teaching methods was hampered by the conservatism of teachers who stuck to the 'cramming and memorization' approach long after this was in any way dictated by large classes and shortage of books and materials [92]. In general, teaching methods tended to be governed by four factors: 'the imperatives of the codes and examinations, the size of classes, prevailing attitudes about the status of children, and philosophies about what education should be preparing children for in adult life' [92: *129*].

The relationship between teaching styles and contemporary attitudes towards children is well brought out by Rose (one of the few authors to do so), who writes that where 'children were to be "seen and not heard" and due deference and subordination were expected, sanctioned by a liberal resort to corporal punishment, teaching was inevitably authoritarian and the learning process regimented' [92: *134*]. The violence of school punishment, and the frequency and extent of it, comes through in so many autobiographical accounts and oral histories as to be indisputable [1; 6; 25; 71; 74; 180]. Nor was it just a matter of violence through slapping, being hit with the ruler or the cane and miscellaneous roughness. Equally hurtful, in a different way, was the teachers' resort to sarcasm as a disciplinary tool [6: *127*]. No wonder, then, that one of the common themes of autobiographies 'is the dislike of school, the punishment and the constant fear of teachers' [1: *152*].

And yet, in Hurt's view, 'to say that the cane was used excessively in the elementary schools and that the magistracy was unsympathetic to the complaints is to judge the past by the standards of the present' [63: *164–5*]. He reminds us of the brutality of society at the time: public executions until the 1860s and flogging in the army until 1881. But this type of argument has difficulty in explaining the presence of those individuals who *did* protest at the brutality of the times, and who, while in positions of power and authority, nevertheless refrained from indulging in the practices. For example, there were teachers who did not resort to the cane; inspectors from the Education Department who protested against its excessive use and tried to dissuade teachers; the membership of pressure groups such as the Humanitarian League who opposed all cruel punishments; many socialist members of school boards; the minority of parents who complained; and the likes of Sir John Gorst, the Tory reformer. Such examples prove that it is not simply a question of applying 'the standards of the present', since these standards were obviously shared by many people in the past.

Children were not always passive in the face of violent and authoritarian discipline. They might attack the teacher, go absent, or indulge in acts of petty vandalism in the school. In their research, Stephen Humphries and Dave Marson discovered pupils' strikes at over a hundred schools between 1889 and 1939 [25; 181]. The two most strike-prone years were 1889 and 1911, both of which were also times of severe industrial unrest. The 1911 strike, which occurred during an unusually hot summer, was the largest on record. It began in south Wales and before being brutally crushed, as were all the others, spread to hundreds of schools throughout sixty-two towns as children picketed and marched through the streets with a set of demands for the abolition of homework and the cane, better heating, shorter hours, free meals and the lowering of the school leaving age.

Humphries portrays the strikes as 'a defiant gesture of protest by working-class children and their parents against the authoritarian, bureaucratic and centralized structure of schooling' [25: 92]. This is to underestimate the role played by the general hostility of adults, regardless of class, to children, and the shared sympathies among adults concerning disciplinary problems. There is little evidence that working-class parental objections to corporal punishment in schools were objections to violence towards children *per se*, rather they were to teachers acting *in loco parentis*. Moreover, it seems that the most active strike-breakers were often mothers [181]. In general, it is much more likely that parents often made use of the law and its oppressive institutions in order to reinforce domestic discipline [72: *161–2*]. Unsurprisingly, then, on the basis of autobiographical evidence, John Burnett concludes that 'a pupil punished at school would receive a supporting beating at home' [1: *155*].

The majority opinion among scholars is that during the period 1870–1918, schooling was a fairly miserable experience for children. This view, however, has been challenged by Jonathan Rose who, through the use of oral interviews, argues against the negative image of teachers and schooling. He claims that a statistical analysis of his respondents' views suggests that the majority (approx 66.5 per cent) had a positive attitude towards school and that they liked their teachers. Nevertheless, 60 per cent of respondents were happy to leave school. Girls were more likely to enjoy school and regret leaving. However, where corporal punishment was concerned, of the 75 per cent who made a comment, 30.6 per cent thought it had been 'too severe', 14.7 per cent described it as 'strict but fair'; while 29 per cent remembered little or no physical violence [182]. Needless to say, a great deal depends on how these figures are interpreted. But given the predisposition of adults in British culture to accept the corporal punishment of children as morally justifiable, the fact that one-third of (adult) respondents thought it had been 'too severe' does seem to indicate a negative rather than a positive image of their school days in this respect.

With reference to the inter-war period, Philip Gardner has conducted an oral survey among those who were young teachers at the time in order to assess the extent and nature of corporal punishment and the teachers' attitudes towards its use. Gardner begins by observing that in addition to being overcrowded, classrooms were often 'fetid and sometimes squalid . . . where the risks from infection or infestation were never far distant'. Such an atmosphere seems to have kept teachers and pupils apart, for there was a 'deep gulf separating teachers from taught, preventing any kind of emotional closeness'. One interviewee recalled, 'In those days [the children] only had surnames; you didn't know their Christian names'. Above all else, the distance between the teachers and the children 'was a product of the dread of losing control over a class'. However much young teachers may have disliked corporal punishment, many came to regard it as both necessary and unavoidable, and gradually became 'inured to, and dispassionate about it'. Even years later, in recollecting for Gardner, if they were 'sometimes reticent or uneasy, they were never apologetic'. And though they might have disapproved of colleagues who were regular and vicious beaters, they nevertheless gave them professional respect. Women, however, as teachers in boys' schools (where generally the cane was far more frequently used than in girls'), were much more likely to intervene or try to protect the children in their class, while at the same time accepting that there was a place for legitimate corporal punishment.

Indeed, very few of the teachers in the survey entirely renounced the use of the cane, the ruler or slapping. But one or two did [180: *145–63*]. Gardner's survey is useful in providing teachers with a voice on the matter of physical punishment, and while he reiterates the well-known justification, namely, overcrowding, large classes and the paramountcy of maintaining discipline, he never really investigates the claim made by Pamela Horn that such punishment was attributable partly to a belief in the need to 'inculcate self-control and orderliness in new generations, even if this meant repressing normal childish instincts' [183: *264–5*].

Of course, it would be wrong to suggest that all children hated school. Robert Roberts found school to be 'delightful. So did all my siblings, and we blubbered and complained if anything occurred to stop attendance' [184: *141*]. According to John Burnett, happy school experiences recorded in autobiographies (which appear to have been relatively infrequent) were 'usually associated with a kind and able teacher who develops a child's imagination as well as affection' and with 'achieving some success in the school such as winning prizes' [1: *156*]. This is not surprising. It is more than likely that obedient, attentive, conscientious, cooperative and clever children found school reasonably enjoyable, if only because they rarely incurred the teacher's wrath. Successful pupils are always popular in the staffroom since their performances make for professional satisfaction while at the same time enhancing teachers' career prospects.

Change in disciplinary methods was gradual, and at first was more or less confined to the primary sector. Progressive education comprised many different strands, but in general it favoured a 'child-centred' approach to teaching with the emphasis on creative effort, self-regulated learning and a variety of informal techniques. It was in independent 'progressive' schools that the most far-reaching and 'outrageous' experiments occurred. Gradually throughout the inter-war period the new ideas and methods seemed 'more and more to fit both the well-publicized theories of the psychologists and the possibilities of the elementary school' [169: *401*]. It was not that such ideas gained widespread conscious acceptance, at least not until the late 1940s. Rather it was that as a 'tendency of thought' the influence of child-centredness 'lay in the slow, but eventually almost universal, acceptance of childhood as a stage of life with values of its own, and of the interests of children as being a relevant criterion of good teaching' [185: *60*; also 174; 178]. By the 1950s there was more free expression and creativity in the classrooms; more trips and walks; fewer rigid rules and less corporal punishment. In 1973 the Inner London Education Authority banned corporal punishment in its primary schools. But from the late 1970s, under the gathering storm of widespread public disappointment at the failure of the welfare state to solve Britain's social and economic difficulties, criticism of progressive teaching methods found political favour through the influence of right-wing Labour politicians and the emerging New Right in the Conservative party. In their place came more conservative policies, culminating in the 1988 Education Act with its emphasis on testing, a national curriculum, and commercial accountability procedures [57; 178].

For secondary school pupils the pace of change was much slower since authoritarian and violent regimes continued up to the 1980s. As late as 1977 a survey found that corporal punishment was used in 80 per cent of English secondary schools, while in Edinburgh schools alone the tawse was used on 10,000 occasions in a single term. By the 1970s there were mounting protests from some parents and from sections of the teaching profession (and from children themselves) against this institutional violence [186], but it was probably the threat from the European Court of Human Rights that finally forced the government to abolish corporal punishment in state schools in 1986. During these years, the comprehensives, as they gradually replaced grammar and secondary schools, were slowly introducing a strand of liberalism into the sector in that they pioneered closer and more informal relationships between pupils and teachers with new teaching methods and greater use of pupils' self-expression and exploration of their own environment [71]. Yet, as Lawson and Silver wisely caution: 'Change has always to be kept in perspective. In very many schools the developments of the 1950s and 1960s made little or no impression' [169: *432*; *438–47*]. Perhaps not until the 1980s could it be claimed with any certainty that 'children at school no longer live in daily fear and dread of their teachers, worried that the slightest spark of imagination and creativity might result in the cane or the tawse' [71: *113–15*].

6
Children's leisure

First, what is meant by 'leisure'? The term is understood here as the time 'which lies outside the demands of work, direct social obligations and the routine activities of personal and domestic maintenance'. The use of this time 'is characterised by a high degree of personal freedom and choice'. Recreation, which can also be used as a specialist term, but is included here as part of leisure, is taken to mean 'those activities and interests that form the typical occupations of leisure time' [187: 6].

Such a definition, however, does not take us very far with reference to children's leisure for, as James Walvin has remarked, despite being a crucial feature of their lives, it has been ignored by historians and left to the antiquarian and folklorist [188: 228]. And John Springhall reminds us that it is an oversimplification to examine leisure solely by focusing on social class, since what is often of equal importance has been 'the position of the individual in the life-cycle' [189: 109–10]. All the same, it is 'undeniable that whatever one's actual age, the choice of leisure activities available in the past was predominantly defined and circumscribed by social class', by regions and by the division between urban and rural areas [189: 113; 1: 240].

On the other hand, it is most likely that from the early twentieth century onwards a 'common culture' was gradually emerging for a number of reasons: the continuing process of urbanization, the rising standard of living, rapidly developing technologies in communications, the growth of literacy leading to a national audience for magazines, comics and books, the development of the cinema as the principal form of popular commercial entertainment, the coming of the radio (1922), the mass production of toys, games and dolls from the inter-war period, the impact of television from the 1960s and, from the 1980s, that of video films and computer games. These developments point to what is universally seen as the consumer revolution [67: *260*], namely, the ability of all classes, genders and age groups to purchase through greater spending power specially produced commodities for the purposes of their recreation.

But the emergence of a 'common culture' for children's leisure, together with their part in the consumer revolution, should not be exaggerated. Class and gender divisions remained in areas like choice of reading matter, category of films and television programmes viewed, range of toys and games purchased and, perhaps most distinctively, with the popularity among middle-class parents of organized and supervised out of school 'educational' activities, usually for girls: ballet, music, singing, drama and horse riding – even if over the last twenty years or so these recreations have become more classless. Boys were and are much more likely to be involved in sporting activities.

Leisure activities provided by school, religious, voluntary and municipal authorities

Given that our period saw the beginning and final acceptance of compulsory schooling, it is worth thinking about the effects of school attendance on the time pattern of childhood. Anna Davin remarks that for working-class children in the late nineteenth and early twentieth centuries, 'work and responsibility were not the separate province of adults, but co-existed with growth, with play and with school' [6: *85*]. Once compulsory schooling began, a minority of children who had been more or less full-time wage earners found that the school imposed a new timetable upon their lives. They were rapidly designated as school pupils who spent their time unequally divided between attending school, wage earning before and after school, doing domestic chores, caring for younger siblings and 'playing' [6; 8; 9; 72]. Even those pupils who had never been wage earners, especially the younger ones, now found that the school day imposed a framework on their time, dividing it into at least two categories: 'work' and 'play'. Thus the school created (very gradually in the case of the poor) a timetable 'which set a novel pattern of leisure and play' [2: *297*], although this only became meaningful for children growing up after, say, 1914, who found that they had more time for themselves [190: *198*].

One feature of this new pattern was the introduction of compulsory school sports, mainly for boys, usually in the form of team games. The omnipotence of this type of 'educational' activity is now so much taken for granted that we have to remember that as a way of organizing children's leisure, it began to develop only in the late 1880s. Following the lead of the public schools, games were incorporated throughout the state system into a systematized ethos which preached the virtues of the 'team spirit': loyalty, bravery, manliness, selflessness and honour – summed up in the concept of *character*. Both the concept and the playing of the games had two important long-term consequences: first, 'sport' was portrayed as primarily a masculine activity, expressing what were held to be masculine virtues and, second, another dimension was added to the process of controlling children's (mainly boys') leisure time for the organized nature of the games was a new experience, one that would prove to be almost inescapable in its effects. However, despite the emphasis on the relationship between boys and games, middle-class schools in particular looked to sports to improve girls' health and child-bearing potential, to stimulate study while counteracting over-strain, to teach moral qualities and to aid discipline [2; 75; 188–9; 191–3].

Many of the adult-sponsored children's leisure activities, both inside and outside school, were provided in the nineteenth-century tradition of making working-class recreation, which was seen as wild and disordered, more 'rational'. The process was part of the middle-class civilizing mission [187; 194–5]. As the century wore on so more and more attention was focused on young people's leisure. Where children were concerned in the late Victorian and Edwardian periods, there was little problem with the younger ones, many of whom would be controlled by their mothers and would attend Sunday school and the affiliated Band of Hope temperance movement. Like many forms of children's leisure, these organizations served a domestic purpose in that they gave parents a couple of hours of privacy. Their high membership, over five million and three million respectively in 1906, undoubtedly owed more to parental authority, the free annual trips to the seaside, the moralistic magic lantern shows and stage sketches than to juvenile religious fervour [1; 71; 76; 189]. (One of the major changes in children's recreation has been the gradual decline of the role played by religion, certainly by the 1920s.) Older children, however, especially boys who had left school at twelve or thirteen, proved to be more difficult. Hence the establishment of the uniformed youth movement, usually associated with religious denominations. The best-known organizations were the Boys' Brigade (1883), the non-denominational Boy Scouts (1908) and the Girl Guides (1910). In addition, there were also hundreds, probably thousands, of boys and girls clubs, providing a variety of activities, often run by local churches. The bulk of the membership was adolescent, but occasionally younger members were catered for in junior branches [1; 71; 76; 189; 195–6].

Apart from schools and religious and voluntary organizations, the oldest providers of leisure facilities were local councils which, by the 1880s were providing art galleries, parks, museums, libraries and swimming baths, all of which children made use of from time to time. In the inter-war period, the 'fresh air movement' sponsored the development of playing fields and municipal playgrounds, which provided a variety of sports and play equipment – all designed to encourage safe and healthy activities. But children sought to impose their own morality, notably through harassing the attendant or the keeper, known as the 'parkie' [71]. After 1945 there was an ever increasing tendency to regularize and organize recreation in open spaces. So popular had adventure playgrounds become – at least with adults – that in the late 1970s, the Opies caustically noted that having cleared away spaces and parklands, the fashion was 'to set aside other places, deposit junk in them, and create "Adventure Playgrounds" . . . the equivalent of creating Whipsnades for wild life . . . the next stage is to advertise . . . for Play Leaders at 32/-, for 2½ hours . . . The provision of playmates for the young has become an item of public expenditure' [191: *16*; also 195]. One purpose behind these schemes, as with all the municipal amenties, was the attempt to 'quite deliberately . . . enforce a certain standard of behaviour' [194: *324*; also 37]. How successful they were is debateable, but they certainly sharpened 'the division between the worlds of adults and children' [197: *73*].

Outdoor play

The late Edwardian years were probably the last to witness a clear division between public forms of rural and urban recreation for children, though, of course, the pace at which the division faded varied from region to region under the influence of urbanization. In the main, the countryside had provided a different environment for outdoor games – epitomized by the glorious spaciousness of commons, woods and meadows – from that of streets in towns and cities. Rural children, besides playing hiding and chasing games such as 'fox and hounds', 'sheep come home' and 'a night's lodging', would spend time birdnesting, climbing trees, damming streams and cruelly harassing small animals. Much of their leisure was seasonally determined as with skating, sledging and snowballing, and going to the annual travelling fair and zoo [71].

Despite the anecdotal mutterings of successive generations to the contrary, nineteenth-century outdoor games – both rural and urban – continued up to the Second World War and beyond. One of the main structural reasons for the persistence of these games lay in the fact that in most working-class homes there was little free room indoors in which to play, so that 'playing out' was a vital feature of the social organization of domestic space. This in turn was essential for helping to harmonize parent-child relationships through providing parents with privacy and a quiet time; and it still is in the homes of the poor, although probably toddlers play out far less frequently nowadays than in the past [29, *iii*]. Thus games, besides affecting children, also serve to influence the network of spatial and personal relationships involving their parents and other adults [37].

In urban areas street activities were more popular: hopscotch, swinging on lamp-posts, five-stones and door knocking. Here, too, there was what Walvin calls an 'informal calendar of games and songs' which produced different games at different times of the year without any apparent planning. Some games and toys, however, were common to children of all areas: for example, hoops, kites, tops, marbles and football (country boys used a pig's bladder as the ball) and cricket. Others were particular to a region or a locality. In London, for instance, street games were more numerous and different from those played in the north; in Leeds there was a local form of tin-can football known as 'kick out can'; in northern mining villages boys played 'knurr and spell' and 'nipsy', which involved using a pickshaft to hit a moving object. There was also a certain amount of gender division, particularly in skipping and rhyming games, and more so in London than elsewhere [1; 2; 75; 179; 188; 191].

With the spread of better housing from the 1920s onwards, many with gardens, space became less of an issue for a growing number of families. Yet the renewal of urban England during the 1950s and 1960s with the building of new suburbs, new towns and high rise blocks not only did away with the old bomb sites and shelters that remained from the wartime blitz and which had been enormously popular play areas, but also altered the layout of streets, and increased the amount of vehicular access. Consequently, children were more confined than in the past. Even so, probably up to the early 1970s, if not later, the street was still a principal arena of social activity [69; 189; 195].

Thereafter, however, 'out of doors' faced serious competition for the working-class child's loyalty from television, the video and supervised recreation such as local football teams, swimming and athletic clubs, piano lessons, dancing class, and so on. Nowadays, not only is children's leisure time more organized by parents, but cities are seen to represent a threat to children from cars and from dangerous adults, even though the figures for road accidents were much higher in the 1930s and children are far more at risk from adults whom they know than from strangers. None the less, fewer children than ever are allowed out on their own either to travel or to play, and many researchers fear that they have fewer opportunities to learn about local geography, distance, time, climate and the reading of street names and signs and, therefore, are becoming less independent and less confident about their abilities. Moreover, as Colin Ward, the environmentalist, has written, there is a tendency to see 'outdoor' children as up to no good, while the indoor child is felt to be out of mischief. All these developments may be bringing about, or may already have brought about, a subtle change in age relations, for it is worth remembering that outdoor play was often not only a form of exploration, but also, for example, through 'daring' games, a form of protest as part of the conflict with adults. In fact it has been suggested that restrictions on children's street-life may well have led to the postponement of this protest through to the antisocial behaviour of some teenagers [1; 25; 191; 197–201].

The cinema

The growth of commercial recreation brought changes in the kind of recreation available. After 1870 the music-halls replaced 'penny gaffs' in popularity among older children and adolescents, and soon the cinema, probably the most influential of all commercial entertainments, was to eclipse the music hall; so much so that after 1918, it was estimated that up to 30 per cent of British audiences were aged under seventeen. It is well known that 'the films' brought forth a great tidal wave of condemnation from religious, educational and legal spokesmen who claimed that they induced delinquency and damaged eyesight and nerves. Notwithstanding all the criticisms, picture-going continued to be a major form of recreation for children up to the 1970s. But what changed from the late 1930s onwards was the emphasis on producing films that were thought suitable for children, primarily through outlets such as the Odeon Children's matinées, with club songs, badges and competitions, and the founding of the Children's Film Foundation (1951), with its emphasis on the making of wholesome entertainment [189; 202]. There is, however, some disagreement among cultural historians as to whether films in general were an instrument of 'social control' in promoting social consensus [202], or whether they simply followed popular tastes [203–4]. By the 1970s another change was well under way as the Saturday cinema matinee was challenged by Saturday morning children's television programmes, which drew much of their content from the world of pop music and increasingly from soap operas. Around the same time, Hollywood accelerated the trend in evidence since the 1950s by producing big budget films with children very much in mind but intended for the whole family, and often linked to merchandising promotions for toys, games and thematic decorations of children's bedrooms. By the late 1980s these films, and others which were carefully targeted at younger children, had found a new mass outlet through the weekend video. The latter period was clearly distinguished by the overlap between the films, Saturday TV, soap operas, videos, pop music and to a certain extent designer-label clothes as 'leisure' absorbed these market-oriented products, merging them, together with 'shopping', into a kind of seamless cultural form. All in all, where children are concerned, this may well turn out to be a profoundly significant shift in the processes and objectives of social education and of social values.

Literature

If the cinema provoked anxiety among adults, so too did the growth of certain aspects of children's literature. Compulsory education, with its emphasis on literacy, meant that reading became one of the most popular forms of leisure during the late Victorian years, especially for boys who devoured 'penny dreadfuls', with their bizarre and fantastic stories spread across eight pages. By the 1880s the middle class was denouncing them as trash: 'Bad style, cheap format, excesses of expression, implausible plotting' [205: *13*]. Young readers appeared to be undermining 'culture' by choosing to read that which was felt to threaten the value of literature itself. In order to appreciate this concern, it has to be remembered that bour- · geois society placed a very high value on the improving qualities of 'culture', especially for the working class. Now, it was alleged, at a time of economic, social and political unrest, compulsory schooling through literacy was providing these children with the means to go their own way towards indiscipline, criminality and moral corruption [205: *10–18, 32*; 206; 189: *128–30*].

The success of the 'dreadfuls', along with technological developments in printing and the expansion of the retail trade, encouraged the publication of rival papers for older children and adolescents. The Religious Tract Society started *The Boy's Own Paper* (1879), and the *Girl's Own Paper* (1880) which, at a penny a week, were bought by the more respectable boys and girls, as was *Chums* (1892). There were also several halfpenny (working-class) 'papers' (which killed off the 'dreadfuls') – *The Boy's Friend* (1895), *The Union Jack* (1894) and *Pluck* (1894) – which promoted imperialism through stories full of daring and courageous adventures set in an imperial background. The first 'comic' as such was the *Illustrated Chips* (1890), followed by *Picture Fun* (1902), *Butterfly* (1904) and *Puck* (1904) (the first colour comic). In 1907–8 two further middle-class boys' weeklies appeared: *The Gem* and *The Magnet*, featuring boarding-school stories. Surprisingly, (or perhaps not) these stories found a large audience among working-class boys. By the late 1920s, *The Magnet* had a peak circulation of 200,000 a week. Between 1918 and 1939, commercial magazine reading spread among all school children, regardless of social class or gender. The new journals had little of the old religious and instructive content, preferring instead to emphasize drama and excitement. Where girls were concerned, there was a greater emphasis on the *school* girl, as witnessed with the new publications, the *School Friend* (1919), the *Schoolgirls' Own* (1921), the *Schoolgirls' Weekly* (1922) and several others. But not everyone approved of the political values being offered to young people. In 1939, George Orwell, the socialist intellectual and writer, wrote a famous essay describing the boys' weeklies as racist, snobbish and conservative. It was an important critique since it drew attention to the representation of 'masculinity' presented to boys as being more or less governed by right-wing ideologies of nationalism and supremacism [189: *128–33*; 190: chapter 8, *167–80, 183*; 205: *38–48*].

Since the Edwardian period, children's reading material, like so much else of their recreation – both commercial and non-commercial – has gone through different phases, all of them directed by developments in the adult world. With respect to books, these are always either 'educational' or influential in some way; they reflect an ideology and, by extension, didacticism – though perhaps not always as intended [207–9]. The educational and morally improving dimension of 'good' literature clearly distinguished middle-class children's leisure from that of their social inferiors. The decade after the First World War, according to John Rowe Townsend, was dreary. The 1920s, he says, was 'a backward-looking time' with old books reissued and an outpouring of 'second, third and tenth rate school and adventure stories'. Unlike much modern children's literature, the realism of the inter-war years was muted with the feeling that children ought to be protected from gritty realities. From 1945 onwards, however, the problems of the world forced their way on to the printed page, as did growing prosperity and mass consumerism. Authors adopted the motto 'tell it like it is'. In the late 1950s and the 1960s there was a long-running controversy concerning the middle-class emphasis in so much of children's literature and the lack of stories involving poorer children. Children's books were said to be 'reinforcing the existing social structure rather than working towards a new one' [209: *169*]. By the late 1960s social trends such as divorce, financial and sexual corruption in public life, racial prejudice and world events were undermining adult authority. Under the influence of the rapidly developing teenage culture, children's literature found new voices and new themes. And though there was something of a backlash in the 1970s and 1980s, in response to the recession and rising unemployment, both of which encouraged conservatism and orthodoxy, realism (in many different varieties) as a genre became increasingly dominant.

Summing up the nature and impact of children's literature is extremely difficult. Perhaps it will be helpful to draw upon the view of Kirsten Drotner who suggests that magazines should be seen as 'emotional interventions into the everyday lives' of their readers. More specifically, they are 'aesthetic organizers of contradictory experiences', by which she means that as children are reared to adulthood, they are kept at a distance from most of the 'social activities and experiences of their elders'. The appeal of the magazines is that they offer a solution to this exclusion [190: *4*].

Games and toys and the domestication of leisure

Kenneth Brown is rather unusual among historians in claiming that working-class children had access to commercially made toys before the twentieth century. Brown emphasizes the rising standard of living in the late Victorian period which, he says, although privileging middle-class children, made commercial toys more readily available to those across the social spectrum. The more common view, however, is that the mass market did not become a reality until after the First World War [210: *41–2, 55*; also 211: *144–5* and 212: *26*; 71: chapter *3*].

Traditionally middle-class children had much less freedom than their social inferiors as their leisure time was spent indoors, or in the garden, under the supervision of parents, nannies and governesses. The most popular middle-class toys were gender specific and included lead soldiers, porcelain dolls and dolls' houses, moralistic card and board games and improving literature. However, the range of toys for middle-class boys was broadened by the rapid inter-war expansion of manufactured Meccano sets (which started in 1908), Dinky toys and expensive clockwork trains. Similarly, the rise of Woolworths as a cut price department store, in providing less affluent children with widespread access to cheaper versions of commercial toys and games, furthered the long-term trend among the working class towards indoor play, as did the development of suburban housing estates with their front and back gardens [1; 71; 188].

Radio, with over nine million licences held by 1939, accelerated the increasing domestication of leisure, and contributed to changes in the pattern of family life [213–14]. The favourite programme for younger listeners was *The Children's Hour*, which was often listened to in the company of mothers. But 'the wireless' introduced a new dimension to commercial leisure for children through Radio Luxemburg's *Ovaltiney Concert Party* sponsored by Wonderfood, the makers of Ovaltine. The programme inspired the formation of the League of Ovaltineys, with a largely middle-class and 'respectable' working-class membership of five to fourteen year olds, who were supposed to drink Ovaltine every night. By collecting the tin wrappers members could obtain an Ovaltine Badge and instructions for deciphering broadcast coded messages which were guides to numerous indoor and outdoor games [71: *78*]. Family listening continued after the war and up to the late 1950s with variety and comedy shows and gripping serials such as *Dick Barton* and *Journey into Space*.

The progress of domestication was also fuelled by a growing interest in the link between 'playing' and 'learning'. The educational potential of toys had been recognized since before 1914, but it became more significant in the inter-war period when, encouraged by several progressive educationalists and psychologists, toys began to be categorized as either 'educational' or simply 'commercial'. For the progressives 'educational' did not mean fulfilling a role in character formation or reinforcing gender values (both of which toys and games have always done), rather it meant assisting in the development of cognitive skills, particularly in younger children. Thus Fisher-Price toys became popular, as did Lego. The pressure on the market to produce more instructive toys increased during the 1960s, helped by changing ideas on child-rearing, which put a new emphasis on free expression and the incorporation of 'play' into the learning process [215; 210–11]. Perhaps this is an example of the way in which adults, unconsciously, sought to structure 'play', through 'learning', into 'work' [37].

By the mid-1950s large sections of the working class were becoming more affluent as the post-war economy boomed, and with it came a return, on a larger scale and more representative of all social classes, of the inter-war commercialization of children's leisure. For instance, higher incomes allowed thousands of boys to become train spotters, sometimes travelling far and wide to collect train numbers. But the first proper post-war 'craze' grew out of an American film (a portent of things to come) of Davy Crockett, 'King of the Wild frontier', and spawned buckskin outfits, imitation raccoonskin caps and Davy Crockett nougat bars. Other crazes, like the hula hoop, followed, and they, too, were often associated with either films or television programmes.

Moreover, improved housing meant that many children came to expect a bedroom of their own, bringing with it a new sense of privacy and space, and decorated in a style of their own choosing. On the other hand, while affluence brought children these improvements in their lifestyles, in reinforcing the extent of home-based leisure, it also tended to increase the amount of adult supervision and control of their play. Similarly, as the modern toy and games market, with its emphasis on the domestic environment, compels children to play under the parental gaze, so out of door recreation has to a large extent come to be dominated by 'the observance of rules created by adults': for example, ice-skating, pony-riding, five-a-side football, gymnastics, swimming clubs, drama groups and computer games. Exactly how all these developments have influenced children's culture is, alas, not known. [71; 200; 211].

The age group for toys as such is now lower than in the past, up to eleven years of age. Older children prefer bikes, sportswear and computers. But there has been a huge growth in the sale of nursery toys – in 1980 they accounted for 45 per cent of the market. A decade later toys were reflecting the imaginary world of the future with 'masters of the universe', 'super heroes' and 'micro machines'. However, the objectives of most of the board games remained much the same, despite new presentations; dolls and animals also remained much as before, but were now battery powered; and, perhaps most significantly, in most of the toys and games the old ideas of good and evil live on [210: 225–7].

Television

By the early 1960s television was fast becoming the principal form of family entertainment, and its public endorsement marks one of the fundamental turning points in the cultural experience of people of all ages and all social classes. At the time, it was estimated that the average child spent two hours a day watching programmes, which had increased to three hours a day during the 1970s. It is possible that the popularity of television viewing was encouraged by the gradual disappearance of the old bomb sites which, as we have argued, greatly reduced opportunities for outdoor recreation. Likewise, the increasing number of parked cars in suburban side roads and the removal of working-class populations from their old areas to high rise estates had the same effect. The availability of play areas was also lessened in the countryside where more land was turned over to cereal production and mechanization and toxic pesticides made the fields increasingly dangerous for children [71; 191; 216].

It has been suggested that as a result of television bedtimes became a little later, and that less time was given to homework, reading and listening to the radio. More importantly, watching television is alleged to have detached children from their peer group, especially with regard to unstructured activities such as wandering about and casually socializing out of doors [71; 200]. Alasdair Roberts, however, in his sociological study, sees television not as a substitute for 'play'; rather it is a medium through which the nature of play is altered [200]. He rejects the simplistic notion that 'child culture is threatened' in that 'children have become less active and playful, and more restricted or TV addicted than those of the past' [quoted in 200: 66].

One of the fiercest critiques of the alleged effects of television on children's play has come from Neil Postman (an American media sociologist) who holds the medium responsible for the collapse of the 'information hierarchy' so that 'everything is for everybody'. Television, he says, has eroded the dividing line between children and adults in three ways: it requires no instruction to grasp its form; it does not make complex demands on either mind or behaviour; it does not segregate the audience. With the advent of television, there are no secrets and 'Without secrets . . . there can be no such thing as childhood' [41: *79–80*]. Joshua Meyrowitz (also an American sociologist), offers a different, more optimistic interpretation. He sees television as revolutionary because, unlike books, the child viewer can switch from children's programmes to adult programmes without any 'prerequisites' and, therefore, it allows children to be present at adult situations: 'Television thrusts children into a complex adult world, and it provides the impetus for them to ask the meanings of actions and words they would not yet have heard of, or read about, without television' [217: *620*; also 218; 219]. Postman has also been charged with assuming the homogeneity of television as a mass medium and ignoring, for example, children's Saturday morning cartoon programmes. Moreover, although he makes many claims about the effects of television, 'few researchers have been able to isolate empirically . . . "effects" or to attribute changes in children's behaviour to television alone in isolation from other continuing cultural processes' [211: *72, 209*; also 220]. Although these writers, and others, differ in their judgements, they agree that television has been a crucial force in reshaping the world of contemporary childhood.

Continuity in children's leisure

In 1969 the Opies, recorders of children's culture, issued a cautionary warning when they observed: 'It seems to be presumed that children today (unlike those in the past) have few diversions of their own, that they are incapable of self-organization, have become addicted to spectator amusements, and will languish if left to their own resources' [191: *v*; also 198: *v*]. The failure of adults to perceive the existence of children's games, they say, is largely because of the adult failure to appreciate that though children need looking after, 'they are also people going about their own business within their own society, and are fully capable of occupying themselves under the jurisdiction of their own code' [191; *v*; also 37; 200]. 'We had been told that the young had lost the power of entertaining themselves; that the cinema, the wireless, and television had become the focus of their attention, and that we had started our investigation fifty years too late' [198: *v*]. The Opies showed how exaggerated such statements were since they found numerous children's street games – chasing, catching, seeking, hunting, racing, duelling, exerting, daring, guessing, acting, pretending – to be alive and flourishing. In addition there were also team games, party games, scout games and singing games, as well as skipping, marbles, five-stones, hopscotch, tipcat and gambling, all of which were thriving [191; 198]. On the other hand, Alasdair Roberts is critical of the Opies' methodology for comparing two 'suspiciously equal lists of rising and falling games against each other' in order to conclude that overall things are much the same [200].

Where Humphries *et al.* write of games now being played by younger children within the school playground, or being adapted by different ethnic groups [71], the Opies tend to emphasize their unceasing universal importance in children's lives. This is not to say that they saw no changes. By the 1980s there had been innovations in daring and pretending games, which they attributed to 'modern technology, television and current events'. Children continued to play 'last across' in front of trains and across busy streets, but now they also 'ride up and down on top of lifts in tower blocks, hurl rolls of metal foil at high-voltage electricity cables, holding the end of the foil as long as they dare before the two make contact in a lethal flurry of sparks'. And pretending games, 'though mostly based on family life and wars between unspecified opponents, now often enact episodes from galactic sagas such as 'Star Wars'; and world news, as seen on television, continues to inspire its quota of games' [191: *ix*; also 200]. The Opies, then, see children as acting upon their environment in that they bring 'traditional' games to new circumstances, such as television programmes and, therefore, they are actively involved in shaping their own world.

7

Conclusion: disappearing childhood and children's rights?

In looking at the notions of disappearing childhood and children's rights, which in many respects are contradictory, we see something of the ambivalent attitudes that 'society' displays towards children. Nearly all commentators agree that since the end of the Second World War, there have been numerous transformations in the meaning of childhood, and in the experiences of children. Furthermore, many commentators argue that the most profound changes have occurred since the 1960s, a decade that heralded significant developments throughout British social life. The changes affecting children were not all of one kind and certainly did not move in a single direction. There was, and there remains, a constant ebb and flow of liberal and conservative measures and attitudes, which both reflect and influence a variety of age relationships involving children and adults. By way of a conclusion to this book, let us briefly look at two crucial features of these relationships: the proposition that childhood is 'disappearing', and the debate about children's rights.

Disappearing childhood

The wide gulf between the substantial minority of children who are economically deprived and the majority who are increasingly affluent troubles many contemporary observers. Others are equally concerned, if not more so, about what they see as the end of innocence (or the 'fall' of childhood). Important features of this trend are said to be the 'sexualization of the world of childhood from the innocence – and ignorance – of the past to the more worldly wise child of today' [71: *147*]. It also includes the assault on children's values by commercial interests, leading to the hunger for instant gratification of desire [41; 208]. The suggestion is that 'in a commercial, fashion-conscious age, boys and girls are so preoccupied with how they look and dress that they can no longer enjoy mucking about and having fun – that they are missing out on the pleasures of childhood' [71: *147*].

For critics, such as Jeremy Seabrook, this is a world in which young people seem to be both more violent and more disturbed; despite having been given more of everything than their parents could ever have imagined, they appear to be confused and lost and without a sense of direction. [212: *7*]. According to Seabrook, the reason for this personal and social disarray lies in the parental sacrifice of children to the marketplace, so that though materially affluent, they are left in a spiritual void. However, the best known thesis, and the most controversial, was advanced by Neil Postman [41] when he claimed that childhood was 'disappearing'. He argued that this was mainly through the influence of television but also by the use of child models in the advertising of children's clothes and adult products, the tendency of children's clothes to resemble adult fashions, the increasing violence of juvenile crime, and the gradual disappearance of street games as they are replaced by organized junior sports leagues (in America). Drawing upon an old image, he likened access to the world of adult information to being 'expelled from the garden of childhood'.

In such a climate of opinion, as Hugh Cunningham has remarked, 'children become alien creatures, a threat to civilisation rather than its hope and potential salvation' [47: *179*]. Television is regarded as dangerous because 'it places before children images of the good life hardly consonant with the delayed gratification endorsed by Postman and before him by a long tradition within Christianity'. Postman's vision of the good childhood is not one of freedom and happiness; 'rather it is good behaviour, a deference to adults, and a commitment to learning skills essential for the adult world' [47: *180*; see also 220: *81*]. Nevertheless, Cunningham does see a 'collapse of adult authority', which 'took effect at varying rates'. He advances two supporting arguments: the economic, which seems to concern mainly evidence of the growth in parental spending on children, and the emotional, by which he means that parents look to children for 'emotional gratification' [47: *182–5*]. Both arguments contain some substance but, as is shown below, it does not necessarily follow that there has been a 'shift in the balance of power between adult and child'.

The sociological writers John Hood-Williams and David Oldman are in no doubt that childhood is *not* disappearing, since children 'remain subject to authority relations' [40; also 99; 165; *221–2*]. Hood-Williams describes the overt governance by adults of children with reference to Weber's notion of 'patriarchal authority', which means 'the probability that a command with a specific content will be obeyed by a given group of persons'. This Hood-Williams terms 'age-patriarchy', referring to an imbalance of power, control, and resources manifesting themselves through adult control – expressed as a demand for obedience – over children's space, bodies and time. He is not saying that there is an absence of affection between parents and children since 'one of the tasks of some modern childhoods is to be companionable, to be fun, to be loved and loving as well as to meet the more traditional requirements to respect, honour and, above all, to obey' [40: *158*]. Similarly, David Oldman argues that not only do adults have far greater control over the meaning and availability of consumer goods, which subordinates children's choices 'towards consumption patterns that do not seriously conflict with those of adults', but also that in general adult–child relations can be seen as 'class relations' involving children's exploitation [165: *46–7*; also 222]).

These scholars, then, deny the claim that the parental search for 'emotional gratification' has entailed a shift in power towards children. On the contrary, it has positioned children in a similar fashion to the ideal 'bourgeois' wife and mother in her historical role as 'the angel in the home': pampered and loved, an essential ornament serving as testimony to domestic bliss, but subservient to male power. With reference to the other main argument in support of the disappearing child thesis, the heaping upon children of consumer goods, toys usually reach children as 'gifts', and we know from anthropological studies that gifts 'are a very special form of exchange which require their own reciprocities. Gifts are not given "freely". Some return is expected' [40: *162*; also 211]. Thus do the economic and the emotional relations between children and parents connect.

As to whether childhood *is* disappearing, the most recent sociological survey confirms that 'childhood as "separateness" largely remains the dominant conceptualization in modern Britain'. Ultimately, it is difficult to assess the disappearance of childhood thesis 'because of seemingly contradictory trends and a lack of real evidence about childhood itself, as it is experienced and created by children themselves' [223: 55].

The children's rights movement

From the late 1960s, largely under the influence of the 'new permissiveness', revolutionary student politics, feminism, and other radical critiques of authority, a concept of children's rights developed in Britain, and there is now a wide-ranging debate drawing in participants from education, law, philosophy, social policy, psychology, anthropology, and political science [224–29]. The early campaigns focused on 'child liberation' and were heavily influenced by American texts, one of which argued from a feminist perspective that the oppression of women and children was 'intertwined and mutually reinforcing' [230–2]. The essence of the liberationist case was (and is) that children were discriminated against, unreasonably segregated from the adult world, and confined to 'childishness'. The important rights were seen to be those involving access to wage labour, voting, travel, property ownership, choice of guardians and sexual freedoms. Liberationists stress that *all* children should not be judged as incompetent and, therefore, children should have the right to self-determination [227–8]. The liberationist argument is countered by a variety of liberal theories, often known collectively as the 'paternalist' or 'the caretaker thesis' [225–6; 229]. Many proponents of this view agree that children experience unfair discrimination, but go on to claim that they need to be protected until they are competent and fully *rational* (this is a key term in the debate). Paternalists stress that they are making decisions for the child on the basis of what it would choose if it were a rational adult. However, it is important to say that these two views represent a spectrum of opinion, and there are many gradations of perspective among scholars and activists.

Broadly speaking, the 1980s saw a move towards children's rights among professional care workers (and their organizations) and in certain legislative and legal contexts. In organizational terms the initial impetus seems to have come from the International Year of the Child in 1979, which led on to a United Nations Convention on the Rights of the Child and, in Britain, the establishment of the Children's Legal Centre. Since then there have been other institutional developments including *Childline* (1986), the Association for the Protection of All Children (APPROACH), the campaign to End Physical Punishment of Children (EPOCH) and, in 1992, the creation of the Children's Rights Development Unit. In addition, local children's rights officers have been appointed in a dozen local authorities, beginning in Leicestershire in 1988. In 1992 the Labour Party's manifesto promised a Minister for Children and a Children's Rights Commissioner, and the Liberal Democrats recommended lowering the voting age to sixteen. The drift in favour of a greater sensitivity to children's rights was also evident in the path-breaking legislation prohibiting corporal punishment in state schools and in local authority children's homes from 1986 onwards. In 1985 came the *Gillick* judgment. Mrs Gillick was a Catholic mother of a large family who took the DHSS to court over its circular allowing doctors to give contraceptive advice to under-age girls. The judgment extended the argument for the autonomy of young adolescents when Lord Scarman stated that 'parental rights yield to the child's right to make his own decisions when he reaches a sufficient understanding and intelligence to be capable of making up his own mind on the matter requiring decision'. Furthermore, and perhaps most significantly, the 1980s also saw a much greater commitment on the part of children's organizations, such as the NSPCC and Barnardo's, to a wide variety of children's rights, including their freedom from emotional abuse and all forms of physical punishment.

However, despite the British government's finally agreeing in 1991 to be bound by the UN Convention on the Rights of the Child (with certain provisos), since the end of the 1980s there have been a number of legal setbacks, some of which may well be associated with the public backlash against children after the murder of James Bulger by two boys. The two most infamous newspaper headlines were: 'Born to murder' (*Today*) and 'How do you feel now you little bastards?' (*Daily Star*). Bob Franklin explains this reaction by its opposition to 'an earlier mythical, cultural construct of the child as the personification of innocence and purity' [228: 5, also 233]. Ideologically, says Franklin, children 'have become the focus of a moral panic' in which, as usual, the media have played a vital role. The government is now less inclined to rehabilitate young offenders; the courts give less attention to the child's voice in their proceedings; and there is less official enthusiasm for limiting the freedom of parents to physically punish their children (such punishment is prohibited in Sweden, Finland, Austria, Denmark, Norway and Cyprus). Moreover, in March 1994 the High Court ruled against a local authority in support of a childminder's right to 'smack' children in her care (with their parents' permission). There have also been a number of legal decisions that constitute something of an 'interpretational backlash' against the *Gillick* ruling, though the situation is less than clear [234].

In a review of children's rights as set out in the UN Convention, and how English law measures against them, Michael Freeman, a leading liberal advocate, found that where the best interests of the child as regards rights of participation, abuse and neglect, freedom of expression, thought, conscience, religion, association and privacy, adoption, and health services are concerned, 'complacency about children's rights in England is totally misplaced' [235]. With this in mind, it is appropriate to conclude this book by noting that a recent philosophical study of the debate has reiterated the well-known belief that there is an inseparable connection between how we treat children and what we, as adults, think of ourselves. To that extent, writes David Archard, 'the oft-repeated claim that its treatment of children says most about a society expresses a deep truth' [225: *170*].

Bibliography

Place of publication is London unless otherwise stated.

Introduction

[1] John Burnett (ed.), *Destiny Obscure. Autobiographies of Childhood, Education and Family from 1820s to the 1920s*, 1982. Essential reading.

[2] Eric Hopkins, *Childhood Transformed. Working-Class Children in Nineteenth-Century England*, Manchester, 1994. Informative and useful.

[3] Olwen Hufton *et al.*, 'What is women's history?' in Juliet Gardiner, (ed.), *What is History Today . . . ?*, 1988.

[4] Elizabeth Fox-Genovese, 'Placing women's history in history', *New Left Review*, 133, 1982.

[5] Joan Scott, 'Women's history', in Peter Burke (ed.), *New Perspectives on Historical Writing*, Cambridge, 1991.

[6] Anna Davin, *Growing Up Poor. Home, School and Street in London, 1870–1914*, 1996. Important feminist study focusing on female childhood.

[7] Carolyn Steedman, *Childhood, Culture and Class in Britain: Margaret McMillan 1860–1931*, 1990. Thoughtful and innovative.

[8] Elizabeth Roberts, *A Woman's Place: An Oral History of Working-Class Women 1890–1940*, Oxford, 1984. Useful section on child rearing.

[9] Elizabeth Roberts, *Women and Families: An Oral History, 1940–1970*, Oxford, 1995. See [8].

[10] David Armstrong, *The Political Anatomy of the Body*, Cambridge, 1983. Foucauldian approach; some consideration of childhood.

[11] Karen Baistow, 'From sickly survival to the realisation of potential: child health as a social project', in *Children and Society*, 9, 1, 1995. Foucauldian approach. Suggestive interpretation.

[12] Peter W. G. Wright, 'Babyhood: the social construction of infant care as a medical problem in England in the years around 1900', in M. Lock and D. R. Gordon, (eds.), *Biomedicine Examined*, Dordrecht, 1988.

[13] Cathy Urwin, 'Developmental psychology and psychoanalysis: splitting the difference', in Martin Richards and Paul Light (eds.), *Children of Social Worlds*, Cambridge, 1986.

[14] Nikolas Rose, *The Psychological Complex: Psychology, Politics and Society in England 1869–1939*, 1985. A standard Foucauldian text. Includes many references to child welfare.

[15] Nikolas Rose, *Governing the Soul: the Shaping of the Private Self*, 1990. See [14].

[16] Nick Frost and Mike Stein, *The Politics of Child Welfare*, 1989. Social policy study with historical sections. Very useful.

[17] Robert Dingwall, J. M. Eekelaar and Topsy Murray, 'Childhood as a social problem: a survey of the history of regulation', *Journal of Law and Society*, 11, 2, 1984. Instructive.

[18] Jacques Donzelot, *The Policing of Families: Welfare versus the State*, 1979. Foucauldian study of the family as object of state social policy.

[19] Cathy Urwin and Elaine Sharland, 'From bodies to minds in childcare literature: advice to parents in inter-war Britain', in Roger Cooter (ed.), *In the Name of the Child: Health and Welfare 1880–1940*, 1992. Very useful.

[20] C. Urwin, 'Constructing motherhood: the persuasion of normal development' in Carolyn Steedman *et al.* (eds.), *Language, Gender, and Childhood*, 1985.

[21] Marjorie Cruickshank, *Children and Industry*, Manchester, 1981.

[22] A. Allen and A. Morton, *This is Your Child: the Story of the NSPCC*, 1961.

[23] Ivy Pinchbeck and Margaret Hewitt, *Children in English Society*, vol. II, 1983. Standard Whiggish account of children and social policy.

[24] Jean Heywood, *Children in Care: the Development of the Service for the Deprived Child*, 1965 edn. See [23].

[25] Stephen Humphries, *Hooligans or Rebels? an Oral History of Working-Class Childhood and Youth 1889–1939*, Oxford, 1981. A standard Marxist text. Emphasises social class at the expense of age.

[26] Denise Riley, *War in the Nursery: Theories of the Child and Mother*, 1983. Valuable but heavy going in parts.

[27] Jane Lewis, *The Politics of Motherhood*, 1980. Standard feminist account. Very informative on the history of infant and maternal welfare.

[28] Brian Simon, *Education and the Labour Movement 1870–1920*, 1965. Standard Marxist account.

[29] John and Elizabeth Newson, (I) *Patterns of Infant Care in an Urban*

Community, Harmondsworth, 1965; (II) *Four Years Old in an Urban Community*, Harmondsworth, 1970; (III) *Seven Years Old in an Urban Community*, Harmondsworth, 1978. Classic account by developmental psychologists of child-rearing patterns in post-war Britain.

[30] Josephine Klein, *Samples from English Cultures*, vol. II, 1975.

[31] Geoffrey Gorer, *Exploring English Character*, 1955.

[32] Lorraine Fox Harding, *Perspectives in Child Care Policy*, 1991. A useful text by a social policy analyst.

[33] Robert Holman, *Putting Families First*, 1988.

[34] Jean Packman, *The Child's Generation. Child Care Policy from Curtis to Houghton*, Oxford, 1981. A standard text. Full of essential detail.

[35] Zarrina Kurtz and John Tomlinson, 'How do we value our children today? as reflected by children's health, health care and policy?', *Children and Society*, 5, 3, 1991.

[36] National Children's Bureau Policy and Practice Review Group, *Investing in the Future: Child Health Ten Years After the Court Report*, NCB, 1987.

[37] Allison James, *Personifying Children: Identities and Social Relationships in the Experience of the Child*, Edinburgh, 1993. Important anthropological study.

[38] Jenny Hockey and Allison James, *Growing Up and Growing Old*, 1993. Stimulating interdisciplinary study.

[39] Dimitra Makrinioti, 'Conceptualization of childhood in a welfare state: a critical reappraisal', in [221]. Sociological essay.

[40] John Hood-Williams, 'Patriarchy for children: on the stability of power relations in children's lives', in Lyne Chisholm *et al.* (eds.), *Childhood, Youth and Social Change: A Comparative Perspective*, 1990. Important essay. Thoughtful and provocative.

[41] Neil Postman, *The Disappearance of Childhood*, 1983. Controversial critique of effect of television on children.

2 New ideas of childhood c. 1880–1920s

(See also 7, 10, 12, 15 and 26.)

[42] Mark Golden, *Children and Childhood in Classical Athens*, 1990.

[43] P. Aries, *Centuries of Childhood* Harmondsworth, 1960.

[44] Shulamith Shahar, *Childhood in the Middle Ages*, 1990.

[45] J. H. Plumb, 'The new world of children in eighteenth-century England', *Past and Present*, 67, 1975.

[46] Lawrence Stone, *The Family, Sex and Marriage in England, 1500–1800*, 1977.

[47] Hugh Cunningham, *Children and Childhood in Western Society since 1500*, 1995. Focuses on Britain. Useful survey.

[48] Harry Hendrick, 'Constructions and Reconstructions of British childhood: an interpretative survey, 1800 to the present', in [49].

[49] Alan Prout and Allison James, 'A new paradigm for the sociology of childhood? Provenance, promise and problems', in Allison James and Alan Prout, *Constructing and Reconstructing Childhood: Contemporary Issues in the Sociological Study of Childhood*, 1990. Pathbreaking essay.

[50] Michael Anderson, *Approaches to the History of the Western Family 1500–1914*, 1980. Excellent survey.

[51] Viviana A. Zelizer, *Pricing the Priceless Child. The Changing Social Value of Children*, New York, 1985. Innovative sociological study.

[52] John Sommerville, *The Rise and Fall of Childhood*, 1982. Survey.

[53] Leonore Davidoff and Catherine Hall, *Family Fortunes. Men and women of the English middle class 1780–1850*, 1987.

[54] F. M. L. Thompson, *The Rise of Respectable Society. A Social History of Victorian Britain, 1830–1900*, 1988.

[55] Hugh Cunningham, *The Children of the Poor. Representations of Childhood since the Seventeenth Century*, Oxford, 1991. Focuses on nineteenth century. Some good sections.

[56] Carolyn Steedman, *Strange Dislocations. Childhood and the Idea of Human Interiority 1780–1930*, 1995. Interesting historico-literary study.

[57] Adrian Wooldridge, *Measuring the Mind. Education and Psychology in England, c. 1860–1900*, Cambridge, 1994. Best account of 'child study'.

[58] Carolyn Steedman, 'Bodies, figures and physiology: Margaret McMillan and the late nineteenth-century remaking of working-class childhood', in Cooter (ed.) [19].

[59] Harry Hendrick, *Child Welfare. England 1872–1989*, 1994. Survey.

[60] Christina Hardyment, *Perfect Parents: Baby-care Advice Past and Present*, 1995. Useful on child-rearing literature.

[61] Roger Cooter, 'Introduction' in Cooter, (ed.), [19].

[62] Gillian Sutherland, *Ability, Merit and Measurement: Mental Testing and English Education, 1880–1940* Oxford, 1984. Important study.

[63] J. S. Hurt, *Elementary Education and the Working Classes, 1860–1918*, 1979. A standard account. Full of useful detail.

3 Parent–child relationships

(See also 1, 2, 6, 8, 14, 15, 19, 26, 50, 52, 60.)

[64] Linda Pollock, *Forgotten Children: Parent–child Relations from 1500–1900*, Cambridge, 1983. Important study. Weighed down by its own thesis that parents have always done their best for their children.

[65] Robert Woods, *The Population of Britain in the Nineteenth Century*, 1992.

[66] Michael Anderson, 'The social implications of demographic change', in F. M. L. Thompson (ed.), *The Cambridge Social History of Britain, 1750–1950*, vol. II.

[67] Edward Royle, *Modern Britain: A Social History 1750–1985*, 1987.

[68] Diana Gittins, *Fair Sex. Family size and structure, 1990–1939*, 1982.

[69] Paul Thompson, *The Edwardians: the Remaking of British Society*, St Albans, 1977. Classic oral history study.

[70] David Vincent, *Bread, Knowledge and Freedom*, 1982. Autobiographies.

[71] Steve Humphries, Joanna Mack and Robert Perks, *A Century of Childhood*, 1988. A popular account. Good photographs.

[72] Ellen Ross, *Love and Toil: Motherhood in Outcast London, 1870–1918*, Oxford, 1993. Excellent feminist study. Subtle and scholarly.

[73] Joy Parr, *Labouring Children: British Immigrant Apprentices to Canada, 1869–1914*, 1980.

[74] Standish Meacham, *A Life Apart: The English Working Class, 1890–1914*, 1977.

[75] James Walvin, *A Child's World: a Social History of English Childhood 1800–1914*, Harmondsworth, 1982. Good introductory survey.

[76] Robert Roberts, *The Classic Slum*, Harmondsworth, 1973. Informative.

[77] Mary Chamberlain, *Growing Up in Lambeth*, 1989.

[78] Carolyn Steedman, 'Introduction' in K. Woodward, *Jipping Street*, 1983.

[79] Jonathan Gathorne-Hardy, *The Rise and Fall of the British Nanny*, 1972.

[80] Pamela Horn, *Children's Work and Welfare, 1780–1880s*, 1994.

[81] John and Elizabeth Newson, 'Cultural aspects of childrearing in the English-speaking world', in Martin Richards (ed.), *The Integration of the Child into a Social World*, Cambridge, 1974.

[82] Daniel Beekman, *The Mechanical Baby: A Popular History of the Theory and Practice of Child Raising*, 1977. Informative.

[83] Steve Humphries and Pamela Gordon, *A Labour of Love: the Experience of Parenthood in Britain, 1900–1950*, 1993. Useful.

[84] Michael Young and Peter Willmott, *Family and Kinship in East London*, Harmondsworth, 1962.

[85] John and Elizabeth Newson, *The Extent of Parental Physical Punishment in the UK*, 1989.

[86] Marjorie Smith, *Parental Control within the Home*, Thomas Coram Research Unit, forthcoming.

4 Children and social policies

(See also 10–12, 14–18, 22–24, 26, 27, 32–36, 47, 55, 59.)

[87] Nigel Middleton, *When Family Failed*, 1971.

[88] Bentley B. Gilbert, *The Evolution of National Insurance in Great Britain: the Origins of the Welfare State*, 1966. A little dated. Useful chapters on early twentieth century social legislation for children.

[89] Derek Fraser, *The Evolution of the Welfare State*, 1973.

[90] Pat Thane, *The Foundations of the Welfare State*, 1982.

[91] Kathleen Jones, *The Making of Social Policy in Britain, 1830–1990*, 1991.

[92] Lionel Rose, *The Erosion of Childhood: Child Oppression in Britain, 1860–1914*. Plenty of detail.

[93] George K. Behlmer, *Child Abuse and Moral Reform in England, 1870–1918*, Stanford, 1982. Best account of founding of NSPCC.

[94] John Hurt, 'Feeding the hungry schoolchild in the first half of the twentieth century', in D. J. Oddy and Derek Miller (eds.), *Diet and Health in Modern Britain*, 1985. Very informative.

[95] Anna Davin, 'Imperialism and the cult of motherhood', *History Workshop Journal*, 1978.

[96] Deborah Dwork, *War is Good for Babies and Other Young Children: a History of the Infant and Child Welfare Movement in England, 1898–1918*, 1987. Plenty of detail. Opposes feminist interpretations of infant welfare.

[97] Nigel Parton, *The Politics of Child Abuse*, 1985. Crucial text.

[98] Bryan Turner, *The Body and Society*, Oxford, 1984.

[99] Berry Mayall, *Children, Health and the Social Order*, Buckingham, 1966.

[100] Chris Shilling, *The Body and Social Theory*, 1993.

[101] Harry Ferguson, 'Cleveland in history: The abused child and child protection, 1880–1914' in Cooter (ed.), [19].

[102] Bernard Harris, *The Health of the Schoolchild: a History of the School Medical Service in England and Wales*, Buckingham, 1995. Standard account. Plenty of detail.

[103] Charles Webster, 'The health of the school child during the Depression', in Nicholas Parry and David McNair (eds.), *The Fitness of the Nation-Physical and Health Education in the Nineteenth and Twentieth Centuries*, Leicester, 1983. The pessimistic view.

[104] John Macnicol, *The Movement for Family Allowances*, 1980.

[105] Stephen Constantine, *Unemployment in Britain between the Wars*, 1980.

[106] I. A. Abt (ed.), *Abt-Garrison History of Paediatrics*, Philadelphia, 1965.

[107] J. Bradshaw, *Child Poverty and Deprivation in the UK*, National Children's Bureau, 1990.

[108] Peter Townsend and Nick Davidson (eds.), *Inequalities in Health: the Black Report, The Health Divide*, Harmondsworth, 1990. Essential for study of child health and poverty.

[109] Judy Allsop, *Health Policy and the National Health Service*, 1984.

[110] Roy Porter, 'History of the body', in Burke (ed.) [5].

[111] John Eekelaar, Robert Dingwall and Topsy Murray, 'Victims or threats? Children in care proceedings', *Journal of Social Welfare Law*, 1982.

[112] Jane Morgan and Lucia Zedner, *Child Victims, Crime, Impact and Criminal Justice*, Oxford, 1992.

[113] Tom Hulley and John Clarke, 'Social problems: social construction and social causation', in Martin Loney *et al.* (eds.), *The State or the Market: Politics and Welfare in Contemporary Britain*, 1991.

[114] H. S. Becker, *Outsiders*, New York, 1963.

[115] Patricia Rooke *et al.* '"Uncramping child life": international children's organisations', in Paul Weindling (ed.), *International Health Organisations and Movements 1918–1939*, Cambridge, 1995.

[116] R. N. Soffer, *Ethics and Society in England: the Revolution in the Social Sciences, 1870–1914*, Berkeley, 1978.

[117] Jose Harris, *Private Lives, Public Spirit: Britain 1870–1914*, Oxford, 1993.

[118] Geoffrey Searle, *The Quest for National Efficiency*, Oxford, 1971.

[119] Michael Freeden, *The New Liberalism*, Oxford, 1978.

[120] G. Stedman Jones, *Outcast London*, Oxford, 1971.

[121] H. V. Emy, *Liberals, Radicals and Social Politics 1892–1914*, Cambridge, 1973.

[122] Lionel Rose, *Massacre of the Innocents: Infanticide in Great Britain 1800–1939*, 1986.

[123] Steven Cherry, *Medical Services and the Hospitals in Britain, 1860–1939*, Cambridge, 1996.

[124] Carol Dyhouse, 'Working-class mothers and infant mortality in England, 1895–1914', *Journal of Social History*, 12, 1979.

[125] J. M. Winter, 'The impact of the First World War on civilian health in Britain', *Economic History Review*, 30, 1977.

[126] J. M. Winter, *The Great War and the British People*, 1986.

[127] Anne Crowther, *British Social Policy 1914–1939*, 1988.

[128] David Armstrong, 'The invention of infant mortality', *Sociology of Health and Illness*, 8, 1986.

[129] D. G. Pritchard, *Education and the Handicapped 1760–1960*, 1963. Standard account.

[130] J. S. Hurt, *Outside the Mainstream*, 1988. Similar to [129].

[131] R. A. Lowe, 'Eugenicists, doctors and the quest for national efficiency: an educational crusade 1900–1939', *History of Education*, 7, 1979.

[132] Harry Ferguson, 'Rethinking child protection practices: a case for history', in Violence against Children Study Group, *Taking Child Abuse Seriously*, 1990.

[133] John Stewart, 'Ramsay MacDonald, the Labour Party, and child welfare, 1900–1914', *Twentieth Century British History*, 4, 2, 1993.

[134] N. Daglish, 'Robert Morant's hidden agenda? The origins of the medical treatment of schoolchildren', *History of Education*, 19, 1990.

[135] J. D. Hirst, 'Public health and the public elementary schools, 1870–1907', *History of Education*, 20, 1991.

[136] J. D. Hirst, 'The growth of medical treatment through the school medical service, 1908–1918', *Medical History*, 33, 1989.

[137] R. Harris and D. Webb, *Welfare, Power and Juvenile Justice*, 1987.

[138] John Stevenson, *British Society, 1914–1945*, Harmondsworth, 1994.

[139] J. M. Winter, 'Infant mortality, maternal mortality and public health in Britain in the 1930s', *Journal of European Economic History*, 8, 1979. The optimistic view.

[140] J. M. Winter, 'Unemployment, nutrition and infant mortality in Britain, 1920–50' in J. M. Winter (ed.), *the Working Class in Modern British History*, Cambridge, 1983.

[141] Charles Webster, 'Healthy or hungry thirties?', *History Workshop Journal*, 13, 1982. The pessimistic view.

[142] Charles Webster, 'Health, welfare and unemployment during the Depression', *Past and Present*, 109, 1985.

[143] Bernard Harris, 'Unemployment and the dole in interwar Britain', in Paul Johnson (ed.), *20th Century Britain: Economic, Social and Cultural Change*, 1994.

[144] Margaret Mitchell, 'The effects of unemployment on the social condition of women and children in the 1930s', *History Workshop Journal*, 19, 1985.

[145] Victor Bailey, *Delinquency and Citizenship: Reclaiming the Young Offender, 1914–1948*, Oxford, 1987.

[146] Deborah Thom, 'Wishes, anxieties, play, and gestures: child guidance in inter-war England', in Cooter (ed.), [19]. Useful for child guidance clinics.

[147] Angus Calder, *The People's War*, 1971.

[148] Ben Wicks, *No Time to Wave Good-Bye*, 1988. Evacuation study.

[149] Ruth Inglis, *The Children's War: Evacuation 1939–1945*, 1989.

[150] Travis Crosby, *The Impact of Evacuation in the Second World War*, 1986.

[151] John Macnicol, 'The effect of the evacuation of schoolchildren on official attitudes to state intervention', in Harold L. Smith (ed.), *War and Social Change*, Manchester, 1986. A critical account.

[152] Bob Holman, *The Evacuation*, Oxford, 1995. Optimistic account.

[153] Peter Boss, *Exploration in Child Care*, 1971. Useful for 1948 Act.

[154] A. Bottoms, 'On the de-criminalisation of the English juvenile court', in Hood, R. (ed.), *Crime, Criminology and Public Policy*, 1974.

[155] John Pitts, *The Politics of Juvenile Justice*, 1988.

[156] Nigel Parton, 'Taking child abuse seriously', in [132].

[157] Michael Freeman, *Children, their Families and the Law*, 1992. Very useful study by a leading legal 'liberal paternalist'.

[158] Robert Dingwall, John Eekelaar and Topsy Murray, *The Protection of Children: State Intervention and Family Life*, Oxford, 1983.

[159] J. Eekelaar and R. Dingwall, *The Reform of Child Care Law: a Practical Guide to the Children Act, 1989*, 1989.

[160] Carey Oppenheim, 'Must the child always suffer?', *The Guardian*, 27 September 1995.

[161] Carey Oppenheim and Ruth Lister, 'The politics of child poverty 1979–1995', in Jane Pilcher and Stephen Wagg (eds.), *Thatcher's Children: Politics, Childhood and Society in the 1980s and 1990s*, 1996.

[162] Berry Mayall, *Negotiating Health*, 1994. Contemporary policy.

5 Children, schooling and the classroom

(See also 1, 2, 6, 25, 28, 40, 57, 62, 63, 71, 72, 74, 92)

[163] David Rubinstein, *School Attendance in London, 1870–1914: a Social History*, Hull, 1969.

[164] David Wardle, *The Rise of the Schooled Society*, 1974.

[165] David Oldman, 'Adult–child relations as class relations', in Qvortrup *et al.* (eds.), [221].

[166] Pamela Horn, *The Victorian and Edwardian Schoolchild*, Gloucester, 1989.

[167] Carol Dyhouse, *Girls Growing Up in late Victorian and Edwardian England*, 1981.

[168] R. L. Schnell, 'Childhood as ideology: a reinterpretation of the common school', *British Journal of Education Studies*, 27, 1, 1979.

[169] John Lawson and Harold Silver, *A Social History of Education in England*, 1973.

[170] Michael Sanderson, *Educational Opportunity, and Social Change in England*, 1987. Clearly written balanced account of the issues.

[171] E. J. R. Eaglesham, *The Foundation of 20th Century Education in England*, 1967.

[172] Peter Gordon and Denis Lawton, *Curriculum Change in the Nineteenth and Twentieth Centuries*, 1978.

[173] Brian Simon, *The Politics of Educational Reform, 1920–1940*, 1974. See [28].

[174] Roy Lowe, *Education in the Post-War Years: A Social History*, 1988. Informative.

[175] Brian Simon and David Rubinstein, *The Evolution of the Comprehensive School, 1926–72*, 1973.

[176] Michael Sanderson, 'Education and social mobility', in Johnson (ed.), [143].

[177] Bernard Norton, 'Psychologists and class', in Charles Webster (ed.), *Biology, Medicine and Society, 1840–1940*, Cambridge, 1981.

[178] Brian Simon, *Education and the Social Order, 1940–1990*, 1991.

[179] Pamela Horn, *The Victorian Country Child*, Kineton, 1974.

[180] Philip Gardner, 'The giant at the front: young teachers and corporal punishment in inter-war elementary schools', *History of Education*, 25, 2, 1996. Original study. Revealing of teachers' attitudes.

[181] Dave Marson, *Children's Strikes in 1911*, History Workshop Pamphlets, 9, 1973.

[182] Jonathan Rose, 'Willingly to school: the working-class response to elementary education in Britain, 1875–1918', *Journal of British Studies*, 32, 2, 1993, 114–38. Optimistic account.

[183] Pamela Horn, *Education in Rural England, 1800–1914*, Dublin, 1978.

[184] Robert Roberts, *A Ragged Schooling*, 1978.

[185] R. J. W. Selleck, *English Primary Education and the Progressives*, 1972. Standard account.

[186] Peter Newell (ed.), *A Last Resort? Corporal Punishment in Schools*, Harmondsworth, 1972.

6 Children's leisure

(See also 1, 2, 6, 8, 9. 29, 37, 41, 67, 72, 75, 76.)

[187] Peter Bailey, *Leisure and Class in Victorian England*, 1978.

[188] James Walvin, 'Children's pleasures', in John K. Walton, and James Walvin (eds.), *Leisure in Britain 1780–1939*, Manchester, 1983.

[189] John Springhall, *Coming of Age. Adolescence in Britain 1860–1960*, Dublin, 1986. Includes material on children.

[190] Kirsten Drotner, *English Children and their Magazines, 1751–1945*, 1988. Thoughtful study.

[191] Iona and Peter Opie, *Children's Games in Street and Playground*, Oxford, 1984, edn. Classic account by 'folklorists'.

[192] J. A. Mangan, *Athleticism in the Victorian and Edwardian Public School: the Emergence and Consolidation of an Educational Ideology*, Cambridge 1981. Standard account.

[193] Kathleen E. McCrone, *Sport and the Physical Emancipation of English Women, 1870–1914*, 1988.

[194] Hugh Cunningham, 'Leisure and culture', in F. M. L. Thompson (ed.), *The Cambridge Social History of Britain 1750–1950*, Cambridge, 1990.

[195] Harry Hendrick, *Images of Youth: Age, Class and the Male Youth Problem, 1880–1920*, Oxford, 1990.

[196] John Springhall, *Youth, Empire and Society: British Youth Movements, 1883–1940*, 1977. Standard account.

[197] Colin Ward. *The Child in the City*, 1977. Standard account.

[198] Iona and John Opie, *The Lore and Language of Schoolchildren*, Oxford, 1959.

[199] Paul Thompson, 'The war with adults', *Oral History*, 3, 2, 1975.

[200] Alasdair Roberts, *Out to Play: the Middle Years of Childhood*, Aberdeen, 1980.

[201] Colin Ward, 'Opportunities for childhoods in late twentieth century Britain', in Berry Mayall (ed.), *Children's Childhoods Observed and Experienced*, 1994.

[202] Jeffrey Richards, *The Age of the Dream Palace: Cinema and Society in Britain, 1930–1939*, 1986. Standard account.

[203] Stephen Jones, *Workers at Play: a Social and Economic History of Leisure 1918–1939*, 1986. Comprehensive survey.

[204] Andrew Davies, 'Cinema and broadcasting' in Johnson (ed.), [142].

[205] Joseph Bristow, *Empire Boys: Adventures in a Man's World*, 1991. Useful introductory chapter on boys' Imperial literature.

[206] Patrick Dunae, 'Penny dreadfuls: late nineteenth-century boys' literature and crime', *Victorian Studies*, 22, 1979.

[207] Gillian Avery, *Childhood's Pattern: a Study of the Heroes and Heroines of Children's Fiction 1770–1950*, 1975.

[208] Nicholas Tucker, *The Child and the Book*, Cambridge, 1981.

[209] John Rowe Townsend, *Written for Children*, 1990.

[210] Kenneth D. Brown, *The British Toy Business: a History since 1700*, 1996.

[211] Stephen Kline, *Out of the Garden: Toys, TV, and Children's Culture in the Age of Marketing*, 1993. Focuses on North America.

[212] Jeremy Seabrook, *Working-Class Childhood: an Oral History*, 1982.

[213] M. Pegg, *Broadcasting and Society, 1918–1939*, Beckenham, 1983.

[214] Asa Briggs, *The Golden Age of Wireless: the History of Broadcasting in the UK*, vol. II, Oxford, 1965.

[215] Antonia Fraser, *A History of Toys*, 1966.

[216] Colin Ward, *The Child in the Country*, 1988.

[217] Joshua Meyrowitz, 'The adultlike child and the childlike adult: socialization in an electronic age', in Harvey J. Graff (ed.), *Growing Up in America*, Detroit, 1987.

[218] Cedric Cullingford, *Children and Television*, Aldershot, 1984.

[219] Patricia Holland, '"I've just seen a hole in the reality barrier!": children, childishness and the media in the ruins of the twentieth century', in Pilcher and Wagg (eds.), [161].

[220] David Buckingham, 'Television and the definition of childhood', in Mayall (ed.), [201].

Conclusion: disappearing childhood and children's rights

(See also 40, 41, 47, 71, 99, 165, 211, 212.)

[221] Jens Qvortrup *et al.* (eds.), *Childhood Matters: Social Theory, Practice and Politics*, Aldershot, 1994. Important sociological collection.

[222] David Oldman, 'Childhood as a mode of production' in Mayall (ed.), [201]. Stimulating.

[223] Janet Pilcher, *Age and Generation* Oxford, 1995.

[224] Peter Adams *et al.*, *Children's Rights*, 1971.

[225] David Archard, *Children: Rights and Childhood*, 1993.

[226] M. D. A. Freeman, *The Rights and Wrongs of Children*, 1983. Liberal/paternalist account.

[227] Bob Franklin (ed.), *The Rights of Children*, Oxford, 1986. Liberationist.

[228] Bob Franklin (ed.), *The Handbook of Children's Rights*, 1995. Wide-ranging collection. Important for contemporary issues concerning children.

[229] Geoffrey Scarre (ed.), *Children, Parents and Politics*, Cambridge, 1989.

[230] John Holt, *Escape from Childhood*, Harmondsworth, 1975. Classic liberationist text.

[231] Shulamith Firestone, *The Dialectic of Sex: the Case for a Feminist Revolution*, 1971.

[232] Daniel Farson, *Birthrights*, 1974. Classic liberationist text.

[233] Chris Jenks, *Childhood*, 1996. Sociological.

[234] Jane Pilcher, 'Gillick and after: children and sex in the 1980s and 1990s', in Pilcher and Wagg (eds.), [161].

[235] Michael Freeman, 'Children's rights in a land of rites', in Franklin (ed.), [228].

Index

New Studies in Economic and Social History

Titles in the series available from Cambridge University Press:

Economic History Society

The Economic History Society, which numbers around 3,000 members, publishes the *Economic History Review* four times a year (free to members) and holds an annual conference.

Enquiries about membership should be addressed to

**The Assistant Secretary
Economic History Society
P.O. Box 70
Kingswood
Bristol
BS15 5TB**

Full-time students may join at special rates.